On the Edge of Effectiveness
Refocusing HR Efforts to Strengthen Organizations

Sam Altawil

On the Edge of Effectiveness

Copyright © 2020, Sam Altawil

Published in the United States of America

190220-01291-2

ISBN: 978-1093482621
Independently published

No parts of this publication may be reproduced without correct attribution to the author of this book.
For more information on 90-Minute Books including finding out how you can publish your own book, visit 90minutebooks.com or call (863) 318-0464

Content

Chapter 1 1
   I.   Introduction 1
   II. Evolution and Purpose of HR 6
   III. Going Back to Fundamentals 10

Chapter 2 134
   I.   Refocusing HR Services 14
   II. Utilizing Maslow's Theory in Practice 20
   III. Selecting HR Professionals 26
   IV. Developing HR Staff 30
   V. Partnerships 38

Chapter 3 41
   I.   HR Effectiveness 41
   II. Mitigating Risks 43
   III. Conflict Resolutions 46
   IV. Long-Term Planning 50

Chapter 4 62
   I.   The Four Fundamentals Approach (FFA) to Designing Leadership Training 62
   II. Human Skills 69
   III. Technical Proficiencies/Specialized Skills 97
   IV. Business Attributes Skills 103
   V. Ethics, Practice & Conduct 114

Chapter 5 127
   I.   Through the Good Times and
        Bad Times 127
   II. Outside the Scope of HR 132
   III. Pitfalls in HR 139
   IV. Glimpse into the Future of HR 147
   V.   Moments of Reflection 152

Acknowledgements 155

About the Author 157

Chapter 1

I. Introduction

At the center of all organizations is the Human Resources department (HR). It is the department which assists the organization with everything that impacts employees and its leadership. This department was designed to utilize different methods for managing, enhancing, and developing workforce experience while maintaining a great place to work.

Some have referred to the HR department as the heart of the organization, undoubtedly because, like the human heart, it has multiple functions that affect the body, both good and bad. When the heart is healthy, the body is healthy and functions effectively. When the heart is unhealthy, it can cause several impairments in the human body. Similarly, HR has several functions that have a direct positive or negative impact on the organization, but it all depends on whether HR is operating efficiently. Many organizations today are still challenged with inefficient HR departments for various reasons, and it has affected their overall operations and delayed success.

When I began my career, I'd never thought of this field called Human Resources. In fact, during my college days, the only time I saw the subject of Human Resources was one course taught in the business department. Since I was a social science major, the course never seemed relevant to take. However, after graduation and pondering the idea of graduate studies, my mother suggested I work in HR while contemplating graduate school. My mother worked in the corporate business world and had good experience with their HR department and thought this was something I could do. Of course, like a good son, I took my mother's advice, and in time, I was given an opportunity to work as an HR Assistant via a staffing agency.

Thankfully, the HR department I began with exposed me to various HR functions, starting with recruitment, benefits administration, and other administrative work. While I learned such functions within a reasonable time, I realized the more in-depth exposure I received, the more complex it became. Naturally, after a time working in HR, these complexities began to make sense, even though there are still misunderstandings and uncertainties, both strategic and operational. One would think a typical process of onboarding new employees would be the same in every organization, yet this is certainly not the case.

Each organization has its own culture, with different types of professionals with different needs. Therefore, there are no one-size-fits-all HR processes. As an example, some healthcare organizations have their recruitment processes tailored to their needs and culture which are likely different than other healthcare organizations. Sure, they share similar steps, but the overall process is different.

Of course, there are many other reasons, such as industry challenges, the ever-changing business and employment world, and management changes. Eventually, every HR professional discovers that there are lots of complexities to HR, and while education (HR degrees and certificates) has been created throughout the years to assist HR professionals, unfortunately, such education alone could not prepare a person for HR leadership roles effectively.

Like many academic professions, there are theoretical ideas and practical ones. In the academic environment, they tend to focus more on theoretical ideas. It makes reasonable sense since the student should be exposed to all ideas, especially foundational ones. For example, students should know how HR began, why and when, as it would explain to students the actual purpose of HR. The challenge is for academics to combine the theoretical with practical teaching, partly because most academic instructors have a full topic agenda covering most of the HR ideas and typically do not have enough time to cover the practical ones.

Additionally, human resource functions typically do not fall within a single academic discipline, like psychology, business, or law. In fact, from a high level, human resources is a combination of all three disciplines (psychology, business, and law). For example, employee relations and conflict resolutions fall within psychology. HR processes and change management fall within business, and compliance and labor laws fall within the discipline of law. This is evident by the various graduate degrees HR leaders obtain during their education relating to the field of HR. Some have obtained a Ph.D. or Masters in Psychology or Industrial Relations. Most have a Master's in Business (MBA) while others received their Juris Doctorate (law) or graduate degree in Organizational Development.

These disciplines cannot be covered in such depth in academics, especially in undergraduate studies or certificate programs but they do cover a general understanding of such disciplines as it relates to the workforce environment.

Moreover, most academic instructors usually teach full time, and they are not currently working as HR professionals. In some cases, they may have never worked in HR, or they worked in a limited capacity in the past, and their knowledge is purely from academics, so they may not have the practical experience to instruct others adequately.

Thankfully, in today's world, there are publications by HR professionals sharing their experience, seminars by experts, and specific training courses which address current challenges in the employment world. Other means of ideas exchange are utilizing professional social media forums, such as LinkedIn, and some even have created workgroups on Skype. However, with all the exchange of knowledge, specific HR training, and education, there are still HR departments that are failing for various reasons, in some industries more than others.

Such failures include but are not limited to:

- Lack of good customer service
- Lack of partnership with the management team (building relations)
- Inability to adapt to the workforce change in the current business environment
- Inability to take calculated risks
- Inability to complete projects

However, before addressing the reasons some HR departments are failing, let us first go back in time and evaluate the evolution and the purpose of HR, which should shed some light on some of the failures of certain HR departments.

II. Evolution and Purpose of HR

Historically speaking, there are a few versions of the actual origins of HR, some attributed to Robert Owens and Charles Baggage in the 18th century when they concluded that people are critical to the success of an organization. Others are attributed to the contribution of Abraham Maslow who wrote the Hierarchy of Needs theory in his 1943 paper, "The Theory of Human Motivation," which essentially argues that humans are motivated by five fundamental needs:

- **Self-actualization:** Personal growth, morality, creativity, problem-solving, etc.
- **Esteem needs:** Confidence, achievements, respect of others, respect by others, etc.
- **Affiliation/Belonging:** Family, relationships, work groups, and overall social needs
- **Safety/Security, stability:** safety, security, health, financial
- **Physiological Needs:** Food, shelter, water, sex, sleep, etc.

There many individuals who have contributed to the evolvement of HR and modern-day practices. It does not take a genius such as Einstein to conclude, after reasonable analysis, that people are the driving force for organizational success.

Of course, in the early 20th century, with the rise of unions, many organizations realized that simply working people like farm animals is not only unethical but inefficient for their organizational progress. Unions became a voice for the laborer, and in time, unions gained political strength, with which lawmakers were forced to create labor laws, and later, employment laws as well. Nonetheless, the relationship between organizational leaders (management) and represented labor (unions) was and, with some current organizations, still is adversarial. One key note is that the purpose of unions is to advocate for better and safer job conditions, negotiate fair wages, and ensure disciplinary measures are completed justly.

However, during the mid-part of the 20th century, organizations discovered (as others have) that people are the driving force for organizational success, and at some point, the shift from personnel departments to human resources departments took effect. Unlike personnel departments which focused on the administrative side of human resources, HR departments evolved to assist organizations with improving people management by maximizing their efficiencies and productions. They adopted motivational methods, such as Maslow's theory of Hierarchy of Needs.

In addition, HR departments began to cover a wider scope of duties and functions. Such functions include but are not limited to employee and labor relations, strategic recruitment, performance management, training and developing, safety, risk management, and staff recognition. Essentially, anything that has direct or indirect effect on employees has fallen under the HR support. In the past, employees would seek help from their union representatives on issues of wrongful pay, complaints about their supervisors, etc., but now, the employee's first stop is their HR department if, of course, the HR department is operating as it is intended.

There are certain departments in organizations that are considered support departments, such as Information Technology (IT), Finance/Accounting, and of course, Human Resources. In a nutshell, this means each department provides services and support to their employees in order for such employees perform their job duties adequately. With HR, there are various services the department must perform (as mentioned previously), which is the reason HR departments are considered customer service departments, and the better service HR department provides, the more satisfied and productive the staff and management.

Throughout the years, strong customer service-focused HR departments have created an engaging organizational culture, which resulted positively in numerous ways: In a union environment, employees rarely sought union assistance since they were receiving direct help from HR, and in a non-union organization, employees would not consider unionizing, since again, their concerns were addressed reasonably swift they and were treated fairly.

Today, HR Departments have become more complex and challenging. There are various reasons for this, such as changes in the business environment, employment/labor laws, and old and new technologies. Some might say there are generational changes which affect the way we manage staff, while others might argue the changes are driven by an upward or downward economy.

Of course, all have some factor in change, yet from a historical prospective, change occurred in the past and it will occur again, so why have some HR departments become more complex and challenging? Why have they been unsuccessful in these areas (good customer service, partnership with management team, adapting to the workforce change in the current business environment, taking calculated risks, and timely completing projects)? This is a tough question to answer because each HR department will have their challenges, and the likely root cause(s) will be different than in other departments, even if they share the same industry.

III. Going Back to Fundamentals

As mentioned previously, each unsuccessful department has its root cause(s), but before beginning the process of evaluations, start with stage 1.

Stage 1: Determine whether the current HR department structure is the right design to serve the employee population of such organization properly. There are several types of HR designs one can research, and based on the number of employees and location(s) of the organization, one can determine a design which best serves the employees.

For example, if an organization is located in one area, one can adequately have an HR department and its staff in one location. On the other hand, if the organization is more complex and has different locations (in-state or out-of-state), then there should be HR support for those employees in different locations. Of course, this is easier said than done, since there are some challenges one must overcome, such as budgetary challenges, space for HR staff (even if it's one staff member), and most importantly, support from the leadership team.

Stage 2: Assuming the current HR design is adequate for the organization, the first step is to determine whether the functions of the HR department is efficiently operating and properly serving the employee population. Whether the

HR department is a small or a large department, certain functions must be processed efficiently, starting with the <u>administrative</u> tasks of HR. Usually that encompasses various job duties from leaves of absence to data entry. The most important part of this evaluation is to ensure process efficiency, that the steps in the process are NOT cumbersome or redundant.

The second step is to determine the strength level of the <u>relations</u> between HR staff (including HR management) with employees and the leadership team. There are various ways of ascertaining the relations' strengths, such as employee survey, team conversation, operational staff meeting, including a one-on-one with key leadership individuals.

The last step is to evaluate prior strategic objectives (if any), the approach, and of course, the results. In this situation, one may discover that, even if the strategic approach had failed, there is a likelihood of lessons learned in this process, and on most occasions, one can build off any positive outcomes from such efforts.

Stage 3: As evaluations become more in-depth, the next step is to analyze HR processes and determine its efficiency. As mentioned previously, processes should not be cumbersome or redundant. Processes should be streamlined, such that it should have the least number of steps to accomplish its objectives — the more steps a process has, the more unmercenary work to be performed. Hence, there should be only relevant and necessary steps to any process.

However, one must first determine whether the process is efficient or not. At times, that's not as easy as it sounds, simply because it's not obvious. For instance, HR processes often are already in place, and it seems to be operating smoothly, yet after some complaints by management and staff, one discovers that such process is inefficient. Hopefully HR leadership has listened to the complaints carefully, and they have begun to evaluate such process(s). HR leadership should attempt to be proactive and create a plan to survey staff and management about their HR processes rather than wait for feedback through number of complaints. It would certainly strengthen the department's credibility.

Suppose upon discovery, there is one process inefficient, and it is difficult to narrow down the cause of the inefficiency. Where should one begin? One tactic (albeit a traditional one) is to go back to the foundation of the process. That means creating a plan as if one is starting a new process from the beginning. Some of the plan's steps might include, but are not limited to:

1) Define the process needed.
2) Determine the actual intent of the process.
3) Begin with the traditional or fundamental approach (i.e. basic HR).

4) Develop steps from the beginning of the process to the end of it.

Of course, one should also customize such processes to fit the organizational culture, if possible. Another approach (and it might be a shorter one) is, after evaluation of the process, make specific improvement/modification, and while the process might still be lengthy, any improvement/modification may make a difference in the long term.

Lastly, evaluating and modifying processes should be part of HR's regular agenda. Nonetheless, I know many will say that, at some point, the process is efficient and complete. At that point, you can rest assured that the staff and management are content.

Chapter 2

I. Refocusing HR Services

While HR has evolved since its beginnings, the results have been positive and negative in certain areas. Regardless of the industry or department size, there are areas of improvement needed, and from a high level, it is sometimes difficult to ascertain these areas.

However, there is one area that rarely anyone questions, and it is the strategic plan set by HR leadership/executives. Generally speaking, the HR strategic plan is a long-term and short-term plan designed to fulfill the organizational objectives. It is intended to identify current and future needs and set tactical approaches to achieve them by utilizing the abilities and strengths of the people of the organization. Of course, since HR is not an exact science, most HR leaders strategize differently, but with some commonalities.

One of those commonalities is shifting some of the HR work burdens onto the managers, staff, and including job candidates. Usually, new technologies are used or creative processes. For example, HR software is used in various forms, such as recruitment, training, onboarding, benefits administration, leaves of absence, and so on. While the majority of the operational work falls within the scope of the HR professionals, there are some tasks managers must complete, even though some might argue it is on a limited basis. Others have modified their recruitment process, in which during candidate screenings, they have shifted the screening questions to complete and submit by the candidates, rather than HR professionals or recruiters conducting phone interview screening.

The main reason for this approach is that today, most HR departments are challenged with being understaffed and overwhelmed by the amount of work. HR leaders are forced to find middle-ground solutions to serve the organizational population and provide reasonable working conditions for the HR staff. Unfortunately, while this seems to be a sound solution to this challenge, albeit it might be the only solution, there are negative consequences.

As mentioned, technology is widely used today in HR, and it is vital for overall efficiency, but not all technologies are created equal. For instance, HR departments utilize Human Resources Informational Systems (HRIS), which is designed to keep track of an employee's information, for example, personal information, payroll, elective benefits, and more. Also, such systems have other modules that are utilized by HR, such as a training module, recruitment, and/or leaves of absence.

Unfortunately, different systems work differently, and they are not all efficient. Many of them are simply not user-friendly, and it requires significant training time for HR staff and managers. The application of the software has too many steps to accomplish its tasks. Constant updates that disturb the daily work or even a substantial update force the organization to stop their administrative work for a lengthy period. Some of the modules do not operate as promised. For instance, during the software demonstration meetings, some companies often promise job completion on a specific module by a specific time but fail to do so.

Additionally, some of these software companies have poor customer service because they cannot listen to their customer's needs. Either they never address the customer's needs, or they provide quick solutions that do not resolve the issues. Therefore, one can easily conclude that choosing the right software product and company is critical, especially since the product is very expensive. Furthermore, to change software products is time-consuming and overall difficult for everyone in the organization.

Rethinking Current Approach:

As we embark on a new era in HR, with new technologies and innovative ways of supporting leadership and staff, HR leaders must continually remind themselves the Human Resources department is a customer service department which serves the employee population and its leaders. This must always be the overall objective of the HR department, yet at times, we have all lost sight of this objective due to various reasons, but as a reminder, happy staff and leaders are most productive to the organization. As we start to rethink our current approach, and as ourselves, how do you make staff happy, and what must we do and where to start? We have to go back to Maslow's Hierarchy of Needs as a base.

As mentioned previously, Abraham Maslow wrote the theory of Hierarchy of Needs in which he identifies five motivation essentials*: Self-actualization, Esteem needs, Affiliation/Belonging, Safety-Security, Stability, and Physiological.* He described it in a pyramid shape, with the largest fundamental need at the bottom to the least (albeit still important) at the top of the pyramid. Of course, from a human need perspective, it makes reasonable sense. Physiological and Safety needs, such as food, shelter, and security, are vital, and some might argue, it is the minimum need for human survival. Affiliations/belonging with others, such as having a family and friends, are important for most, but not necessary for all.

The last two stages of the pyramid are esteem and self-actualization, which focus on achievements, confidence, respect, morality, creativity, self-accomplishments, etc. However, some might argue, while these two categories are important, they fall short of being a human need simply because not all humans desire or pursue the objectives in these categories. If some live at the poverty level, there is likelihood that most of their interest is focused on the need to survive, but that's another discussion.

At some point during the last century, Maslow's Hierarchy of Needs became applicable to the employment environment, especially after the birth of unions. At the time, unions became the voice for the employees/labor because of bad job conditions. Wages were dreadful, which many have argued, was at the poverty level. Moreover, the conditions of the jobs were unsafe. This defies Maslow's largest need for physiological and safety categories. As time passed, organizations began to fulfill the five essential needs and use it a foundation to build a stronger workforce, and it resulted in a happier (excluding daily conflicts) and more productive staff.

There are HR experts today who believe that Maslow's Hierarchy of Needs is no longer applicable for today's workforce, and believe they are beyond this theory. However, while I agree that some organizations have performed great work with their employee and leadership population satisfaction, those who are struggling in this area should consider and utilize Maslow's Need theory as a checklist for reviewing certain HR processes.

II.   Utilizing Maslow's Theory in Practice

As mentioned, Maslow's theory of needs provided us with a guideline and insight into human needs and fulfillment. As we HR professionals attempted to rethink our HR approach and processes, applying this theory in practice should be simple. For example, first, list Maslow's Five Needs on one side of a diagram. Next list the most relevant HR practices that relate to each of Maslow's Needs (see diagram below). After that, begin the analysis and determine whether your HR department has enough processes and functions to satisfy each of Maslow's Needs. Moreover, from future strategic planning, this diagram tactic can be used as a checklist tool to build and strengthen employee satisfaction.

Self-actualization Needs: Personal growth, morality, creativity, problem-solving, etc.	• Is there a culture that promotes and practices ethical conduct? • Does the mission of the organization express strong values? • Does the organization promote and encourage innovation, creative thought, and willingness to give reasonable opportunities for such creativity? • Besides job growth, are there opportunities for personal growth such as educational programs for other positions in the organization? • Does the organization set expectation to solve problems?
Esteem needs: Confidence, achievements, respect of others, respect by others, status, etc.	• Does the organization have employee and management appreciation programs? • Are employees encouraged to appreciate others in the organization? • Do members of the leadership team regularly appreciate their staff?

	- Are teams encouraged to appreciate other team members in the organization?
- It there a culture empowering staff and management?
- Is there a culture of nurturing one's professional reputation?
- Are there recognition programs for exceptional achievements?
- Are there opportunities for job growth to a higher position?
- Is there a culture of taking pride in one's job no matter what the job is?
Affiliation/Belonging Needs: Family, relationships, work groups, overall social needs.	- Does the organization promote work groups?
- Are there team-building strategies incorporated into the culture?
- Are there any organizational activities, such as sports, music, or other?
- Are there ride-sharing practices incorporated?
- Does the organization promote social gathering for their staff, such as holiday and picnic events, etc.?

	• Is the organization family friendly? If so, are the employee benefits designed to be family friendly? • Are there resources for childcare? • Are there policies for staff dating within the organization? • Is there a policy for family members working in the same organization? • Is there a culture of cross-team collaboration within the organization? • Is there a culture of cooperation?
Safety-Security Needs: stability, safety, security, health, financial, property	• Is the organization stable to have a reasonable belief in job security? • Does the organization have a comprehensive safety plan? • Does the organization have adequate security? • Is there a good retirement plan? • Is there assistance to help an employee with purchasing property or finding adequate rentals?

Physiological Needs: Food, shelter, water, sex, sleep, etc.	• Proper wages. Is the organization paying fair market wages by living areas? • Is the work over-cumbersome in that does not allow for adequate rest? • Is there proper life insurance benefit? • Is there a good healthcare plan for employees?

Lastly, there are various ways to utilize Maslow's Needs theory in HR, and this is where creative thoughts must be applied. At the end of the day, if organizations are meeting employees' needs, these employees are satisfied and happy, and, of course, productive, dedicated, and committed to the organization, it still takes the HR department working on behalf of the organization to lead the way to employee satisfaction. This means creating a customer service culture within the HR department and hiring and training HR professionals who possess customer service aptitude.

III. Selecting HR Professionals

If one surveys HR leaders and asks what their ideal HR professional is, I would guess most would probably focus on the technical skills of these HR professionals, and likely would want HR certificates as part of the recruitment requirements. Of course, this is not necessarily the wrong method. It's a very common method, yet the question should be, before beginning the recruitment process, "What are the vision and the mission of the HR department?"

Each department leader should have a vision of how the department ideally must operate. The vision is a department mission, providing overall objectives of the department, and departmental strategic goals, detailing plans of action. Once accomplished, the HR leader must determine his/her staff's needed skills to assist with accomplishing the goals of the department. If the current staff are lacking in certain skills areas, training must be provided. After that, if it is determined additional staff is needed, and it is within the budget, now one can start the recruitment process.

Here are the challenges. As one narrows down the skills needed for the open position(s), one must consider what candidates the market provides. In most cases, the market will not provide perfect candidates since the notion of perfect candidates is whimsy at best. Many organizational leaders waste significant time searching for the perfect candidates and, of course, never find them. Other leaders create a job opening with a description of their wish list skills, deriving from pieces of various excellent employees. Some call it a "Frankenstein" position. Unfortunately, no one finds the perfect candidate, since they do not exist. Rather than search for the perfect candidate, one should search for an ideal candidate for his/her department. Ideal candidates are not perfect, but instead, they bring certain skills that are valuable to the department and/or organization.

As we rethink HR services, let's consider the HR staff needed for a customer service department. Yes, technical HR skills are certainly needed and highly desirable, but what about particular types of behavior skills, specifically in areas of customer service? How does that apply in the HR department? In a nutshell, customer service behavior is the willingness to assist others, which covers a range of abilities from active listening, empathy, clear communication, positive attitude, calmness under pressure, time management, to being professional. For the HR department, staff that is customer service oriented serves the employee population directly, with a humanistic approach.

With direct service, HR staff will complete the task(s) for each employee or a group of employees. On the other hand, with the humanistic approach, it allows HR staff to focus on empowering an employee and assist him/her in solving their issue(s). This approach aids the employee in developing confidence and self-reliance *(See Carl Rogers for Humanist psychology theory)*. Undoubtedly, both direct and humanist approaches are necessary for an HR customer service department.

Naturally, the ideal candidate for this department is one who has both the technical skills and strong customer service abilities. However, recruiting for HR staff in a customer service department (at the intermediate or advanced level) can be challenging simply because there is more emphasis on customer service behavior than the technical skills.

Of course, there are two schools of thought on this topic. One school of thought believes that, given a choice, one should select those with strong technical skills and lower customer service aptitudes (80% technical skills, 20% customer service: 80/20 rule). In this school of thought, they believe that it is simpler to teach, train, and develop those in the 80/20 technical skills in the area of customer service.

In contrast, the other school of thought sees the 80/20 rule in reverse (80% customer service abilities, 20% technical skills). The rationale behind this belief is that there are individuals who are more comfortable interacting with people, and typically, such individuals have a better understanding of human behaviors. They tend to be good listeners, empathetic, and generally are always willing to assist others. Arguably, such traits can be taught; however, the question will always remain. Which is simpler to teach, customer service abilities (especially for those technically sound, but lack people skills) or technical skills for those who may not have strong technical aptitudes? This is something for each HR professional to determine based upon his/her experience, research, and analysis.

IV. Developing HR Staff

By the time one becomes an HR leader, he/she must have a solid, fundamental knowledge of developing his/her staff. The main reason is that HR leaders are generally considered the experts in this area and organizational management relies on their expert consultation. What does it mean to develop someone? Is it to train a person for promotional advancements potential? Is it to advance their skills and improve their overall professionalism? Is it all of the above?

In actuality, it can be any of those: promotional advancement, advancing their skills, or both, simultaneously developing a person for promotional advancement while advancing his/her skills. Nonetheless, there are a few challenges that we must acknowledge. Staff development has to satisfy three needs:

1. Organizational needs
2. Departmental needs
3. Employee needs.

Other factors to consider are resources for training and developing, and lastly, an organization-wide culture promoting staff development. However, is staff development necessary? The short answer is yes. The benefits of staff development are many, from retaining excellent employees, stronger contribution to both department and organization, to creating a succession path to continue the organizational business objectives.

In the field of HR, staff development varies from different skill sets and functions. Of course, the size of the department can have a bearing on the training and development directions. The smaller the department, the more likely there would be a need for an HR Generalists. Commonly, HR Generalists are those who are skilled in various HR functions. While most refer to them as "jack of all trades," they can be a master of one or two functions. This HR person is most likely to be developed for HR management position since they probably make adequate decisions based upon their experience in all functions of HR. However, in a larger HR department, more HR specialists tend to have more of specific HR function expertise such as compensation, benefits, labor relations, etc. Mostly, in such large departments, they support larger staff populations, and specialized HR professionals are needed.

Satisfying Organizational Needs:

Often, I have read or heard from many organizations asserting they have many opportunities for current and future employees. Usually, this is a strategy to attract new talent to the organization, since many organizations know that talented candidates are consistently interested in furthering their professional growth, especially within the organization. Unfortunately, on many occasions, such opportunities are limited, and the choices offered may not be ideal for most of these candidates. The main reason is, for an organization to create opportunities for employees, it has to satisfy the organization's operational business needs, directly or indirectly. For example, as an indirect need, if the organization creates a leadership role in a specific department, usually this would mean they need a manager to oversee staff and assure tasks are being completed. As a more direct need, the organization may decide it is necessary to hire an additional salesperson to help generate more business, hence assisting in fulfilling the direct business needs.

The challenge for organizations is most have the desire and the intent to create opportunities but may not be able to so simply because the business is not driving in this direction. For instance, typically during economic troubles, the business drives organizations into a safe, low-risk mode to maintain operations, and in a good economy, the business will drive the organization in a direction which may not be predictable at times. However, I have seen organizations that forecast future business very well and were able to create opportunities for their employees. Either way, creating opportunities for advancements must satisfy organizational needs.

For HR leaders, this task is more challenging for the following reasons: One, HR is not a revenue-generating department, and any additional staff or promotions tend to be costly for the organization. Two, there are still organizations today which erroneously feel that HR is an administration office that produces little value to the organization. Clearly, there are more challenges for HR leaders to overcome, but it can be done, and it has before.

HR leaders must show (in various ways) the direct, positive impact HR has on organizational operations. The easiest way to think about it is to envision there is suddenly no HR department. Imagine who will recruit talent or manage employees and management's needs for the organization. After that, you will discover a long list of important tasks, which normally support the organization, would plunge and detrimentally impact the business.

[For example, some small healthcare organizations failed to recruit an adequate number of physicians, and since they had limited doctors employed, they could only see a small number of patients, including unreasonably long appointment waiting times. Eventually, patients will seek other places for their healthcare, and it would result in a loss of business. Sooner or later, such organizations could not sustain financial business operations and were forced to close.]

Besides establishing the need for HR, HR leaders must show the value produced by HR, such as managing succession planning to assure continued future business, leadership training to ensure proper management, strategically aligning business goals with people management, etc. Once accomplished, HR leaders can connect the values and needs that HR provides to organizational objectives and needs, and it would at least satisfy the first development need.

Satisfying Departmental Needs:

Departmental needs might be the simplest to establish, since most HR leaders usually know the needs for their department. At times, it can be challenging, especially if department turnover's occurring and/or the department is overwhelmed with work. This is a good time to stop and rethink the overall departmental needs. Moreover, it is also a good time to incorporate HR staff's feedback on areas the department might not be fulfilling due to staffing or other issues. On many occasions, the HR staff may have a better idea of some of the departmental needs, especially since they are regularly working in the daily HR operations.

Afterward, evaluate all the facts obtained and observed and determine the departmental needs. It might be additional staff in specific area or developing existing staff for specific jobs.

Lastly, and perhaps most challenging, is evaluating options such as realistic recruitment, resources for training and development, additional resources like providing other members of HR to assist in the development process. Before beginning to exercise all the options, however, there are still the employee's needs to address.

Satisfying Employee's Needs:

As we look back at Maslow's Hierarchy of Needs theory (specifically Self-Actualization), we can reorganize some people need to achieve. As many professional leaders will discover, not everyone has such need, but only a few. The few who want to achieve and advance to higher or different positions usually have a clear idea of their end goal but an unclear idea of the path to take. This is where good leaders (HR or other leaders) must assist those individuals on the path to achievement and/or advancement.

Typically, nothing as easy as it seems. Sometimes, those who want to achieve or advance may not be the strongest employees in the team, or in fact, they may not have expressed their interest in advancement or any type objectives to accomplish. In such situations, this may not be obvious for team leaders, and such individuals are often neglected. Again, not everyone has the desire to accomplish or advance, so it is proper protocol to give everyone an opportunity. In doing so, team leaders must meet with each staff member and inquire about their goals, ambitions, or any other professional desires.

Most likely, there will be some (if not many) who have higher aspirations to achieve or advance, and now it is up to the leader in weighing all the options and attempting to connect the employee's desires to the opportunity in the department and organization. Yes, this is a difficult task, especially since most employees have different aspirations. However, since this is not an exact science, there is room for flexibility and creativity. For example, assuming there are no opportunities within the organization for professional growth, how do you develop a talented person?

In a nutshell, provide training in areas where this person needs improvement and provide exposure to projects, relevant meetings, and team strategies, and allow participation in all the above. Of course, the risk is that, once this person is developed and there are no existing opportunities within the origination, he/she might seek employment elsewhere, and worse, to the organization's competitor. On the other hand, if organizations are known for developing staff but without internal opportunities, they build a strong reputation as a great place to work, regardless of any turnovers.

Assuming there are opportunities in an organization and its departments, and assuming there are talented individuals who can fill such positions. Naturally, the next step is to place such talented individuals into appropriate available positions. Of course, there must be a process with appropriate steps to ensure fairness for all employees, the right skill sets, and the right behavior needed for each position.

If there are multiple internal candidates for one position, then all candidates must be interviewed in the same manner as external candidates. The selection process should be the same for internal as for external candidates. At times, however, there are situations in which there is one available position for advancement and only one potential internal candidate, yet this candidate may not have the exact number of years' experience needed for the job and/or may not have the exact technical skills. In this situation, the mixture of training (internal or external), exposure to and participation in current challenges and projects, applying mentorship methods, and any other means of assisting this individual to develop into this position.

One key note: There are various ways of developing others and sometimes creativity is needed. Each person learns differently than the other; however, once you find the right recipe for developing, document the process for practical consistencies and future HR staff training.

V. Partnerships

Real HR Contributions are Helping Others Succeed:

The nature of Human Resources departments is to provide services for their organizational staff and its leadership, but the methods for providing services vary from one department to another. One thing all these HR departments have in common is they must help advance the business objectives of their organization through talent management. One method is the Partnership Method, in which HR Professionals partner with organizational leaders on various projects, departmental goals, strategic planning, and resolutions of challenging issues. For some larger HR departments, this is not a new concept given that they have professional HR staff located in various locations, cities, or states designed to support their region. This staffing is usually referred to as HR Business Partners, HR Managers, or Directors of HR operations, depending on the level of experience.

The partnership method is designed to basically assist all levels of leadership with various stages of work challenges and projects. It requires the HR professional to be included and participate in such projects and daily challenges. For leaders, the benefits of such partnerships incorporate direct HR feedback and support on various personnel matters, whether they are union topics, employee training, strategic recruitment and other matters, including but not limited to an opportunity to explore alternative options. For HR professionals, it allows them to stay ahead and be proactive on such projects and challenge. Moreover, it allows HR to forecast and plan for the future. Additionally, with the partnership method, it reduces the unforeseen challenging circumstances or issues which tend to cause reactive solutions which normally are not ideal.

Structure of Partnership Method:

From an HR department design viewpoint and depending on the size of the department in the organization, the structure for partnership should be as follows:

Executive team & Senior leadership	PARTNERSHIP ⟶	Head of HR & Senior leader
Mid-level operational leadership team	PARTNERSHIP ⟶	Mid-level HR management
Staff population of the organization	PARTNERSHIP ⟶	All HR Staff

The head of the HR department/senior HR leadership must develop strong relations with each executive team and directly build working relations (i.e., partnerships). In the same manner, the mid-level HR management must do the same for the mid-level operational leadership team. However, assuming, one has a small HR department without mid-level HR management, then the responsibilities of supporting the mid-level operational leadership fall to the senior leader of HR. Lastly, supporting the employee population of the organization, which will be the responsibilities of the entire HR department. Most likely, there will be more daily HR administrative support for the employees of the organization. This is not to say the HR administrative staff does not support all the leaders of the organization, but the main difference is the strategic partnership that HR management must provide for the overall benefit of the entire organization.

Large organizations typically support bigger staff populations and require a larger HR department, which means larger administrative staff, with several layers of mid-level HR management, but with one departmental leader. The staff and mid-level HR management might be spread out throughout locations in various states or even countries, but ultimately, they are there to support the employee populations directly.

Conceptually speaking, the partnership method can work for any size organization. It is a simple matter of creating a partnership/service/values system tied to the mission of the organization, training and hiring HR staff on those values, and positioning HR team members appropriately to fulfill the objectives of such values.

Chapter 3

I. HR Effectiveness

During the HR department lifecycle, there are **four areas** in which HR must be proficient to be truly effective for the organization.

1) Must provide excellent customer services for the employee populations (see previous discussions).
2) Mitigate risks for the organization, such can include but not limited to, preventing employee legal challenges, exercising fiduciary duties, maintaining confidentialities, and overall assuring compliance.
3) Conflict resolutions, which many refer to as putting out fires.

4) Must provide long-term plans for the continuing future operations of the organization, which can include Succession Planning, Efficiency Strategies, Leadership Development, and other strategic plans to carry the organization to the next generation.

II. Mitigating Risks

In every HR department, there is a sense of caution when it comes to potential lawsuits by employees, in part because the courts are filled with legal employment proceedings, from arbitrations to jury trails. Every year, there are employment law changes and departments spend a significant amount of time and money maintaining knowledge to ensure processes and practices are complaint with recent adaption of the laws.

Somehow legal proceedings occur (even with full compliance) which has many HR professionals puzzled. I remember a colleague of mine mentioned that she and her staff did everything to avoid a lawsuit, yet it still occurred. Unfortunately, this is the reality, regardless of staying fully compliant. The notion of avoiding 100% of legal challenges is misleading. In actuality, by staying fully complaint, the organization is more strongly positioned to defend a lawsuit.

Here is a scenario which illustrates an employee lawsuit even after following full compliance protocols:

- An employee was involuntary terminated for wrongful conduct.
- The employee's manager and HR department followed the proper disciplinary policy and procedures, which

has three disciplinary corrective action steps, the third being the final warning before termination.
- All the corrective action warnings were completed timely and properly with relevant and verifiable facts.
- The employee violated the final corrective action warning which naturally necessitated termination.
- The former employee filed a lawsuit for wrongful termination, claiming several issues, including discrimination (protected class or other).
- Next, HR contacted their legal counsel, beginning the process of evaluating all the documentation and evidence for this case, and determining employee's counsel claim.
- Legal counsel determined organization is in good standing, the employee's claim lacked legal merit, and likelihood of success is high for the organization.

However, for some HR professionals, the facts of this scenario are confusing. Here, we have excellent compliance practices by HR, yet they could not avoid a lawsuit, which, of course, stands to reason for the confusion.

Unfortunately, in this situation, it all depends on the court and whether the court sees some legal merit for litigation or dismisses it as a frivolous lawsuit. At the same time, it depends on whether the organization's legal counsel can strongly argue for dismissal based on lack of evidence or frivolous suit. The good news is, on many occasions, the courts have dismissed these types of cases for lack of legal merit.

One key note to remember is this scenario is not typical. Many organizations are not 100% complaint or don't document issues perfectly. This, of course, makes it more difficult to defend a legal case in a timely manner. The more time it takes to defend a case, the more financial cost it incurs for the organization, which forces a significant monetary settlement. For organizations and their HR department, they have limited options to avoid litigation, and the most we can do is attempt to be fully complaint, document issues properly and in a timely manner, and confidently position the organization to defend employee litigation more strongly.

III. Conflict Resolutions

In my previous experience in the manufacturing environment, I had the opportunity to manage HR in one the most problematic locations in this organization. On my first day, before I could turn my computer on, the maintenance manager and his employee came into my office with a conflict that needed to be resolved immediately, or later today. Of course, I did not resolve this conflict in the same day, but rather within three days. This factual scenario is not unusual for HR professionals, regardless whether they work in high-tech, manufacturing, healthcare, or other industries. People are people and they will disagree with one and another. That is healthy until the disagreement escalates to a conflict. Unfortunately, conflicts will occur in the workplace, and it can be for various reasons and between different parties.

As HR professionals, we must attempt to resolve all conflicts within a reasonable time to keep them from escalating to something far worse, such as lawsuits. One important factor to remember, there are more complex conflicts which can occur in the workplace, such as bargaining unit grievances, harassments, hostile work environment, disciplinary measures, questionable promotions, and more. These types of conflicts require specific skills by the HR professional (employee relations), which include but are not limited to investigatory skills, excellent listening and note-taking abilities, solid knowledge of human behavior, knowledge of current organization's policies and procedures, union bargaining agreement (if applicable), current state laws, ability to decipher relevant from irrelevant facts, and above all, manage time appropriately.

While disputes, disagreements, and conflicts must be resolved within a reasonable time, the beginning process is the most critical. At accidents or crime scenes, law enforcement investigators begin the investigations as soon as possible while evidence is still intact. In workplace situations, the HR Employee Relations professional must do the same and begin the process as soon as he/she can, though, of course, for different reasons.

The main reasons:
1) To prevent disputes or conflicts from escalating.
2) Depending on the circumstances, if investigations require interviewing witnesses, it's best to complete it while the facts are still fresh in their minds.
3) Strengthen HR's credibility with all parties involved by showing promptness and seriousness of the investigative matters, no matter how trivial some might feel it is. (In my personal view, no issue is too trivial, since any issue has the potential to escalate to something severe.)

The next step is the investigatory stage, in which the HR Employee Relations (ER) professional gathers all the facts, interviews witnesses (if necessary), and begins to narrow down the relevant issue(s) that might have violated any policies or law. During such time, some HR professionals consult with legal counsel, or some conduct their own research, if they are able to do so. Thereafter, based on the credibility of the evidence obtained, the HR professional either develops a theory or conclusion of what occurred.

[Note: Investigation status communication is necessary for all parties involved, from the beginning of the investigation, during, and in the final stages of the investigation. Status communication allows parties to receive some feedback (even if the process moving slowly) as to the progress of the current investigation.]

[Another note: If resolution can be achieved anytime during this investigation, then the HR professional must do so with the approval of his/her senior leadership.]

The last step is the final stage of the investigation in which the HR Employee Relations professional determines action and makes recommendations to the senior HR leader and appropriate manager(s). In this situation, the HR professional must present all the relevant facts that are supported by evidence and present his/her analysis of the investigation with a recommendation for action.

Keep in mind this is a general overview of a conflict resolution process many HR Employee Relations professionals manage daily. The job of resolving conflicts can be very difficult, time-consuming, and emotionally demanding. It requires patience, understanding, empathy, and above all, a certain emotional calmness.

IV. Long-Term Planning

In most organizations, any long-term planning is usually designed by the Chief Executive Officer (CEO) or the President of the organization. Where the organization is headed in the future all depends on the vision of the CEO or President, yet even with great future plans for the organization, the CEO recognizes that it cannot be achieved without the contributions of other departmental leadership and their staff.

Departmental leaders understand that they must tailor their strategic future plans to the CEO's plans. From the HR perspective, this means providing strategies for hiring, developing, and retaining top talent to meet the organization's current and future objectives. However, to meet the current organization's goals, the planning phase is easier than planning for the future, simply because the existing business needs are clear and it is a matter of connecting the right talent to fulfill such business needs. On the other hand, future planning requires an elaborate succession plan. In some organizations, succession planning is for senior leadership only.

Contingency and Succession Planning:

The traditional notion of a succession plan is to identify future leaders to replace the current ones in order to continue the business of the organization. Today, many HR professionals and their operational leaders must think beyond the boundaries of this traditional idea of succession planning. As an example, high staff turnovers followed by constant recruitment and hiring have negatively affected the operations of the organization, from inconsistent practices to bad customer delivery and overall operational inefficiencies. Unfortunately, this brutal cycle will continue until operational leaders and their HR partners begin strategizing for staff efficiency. One of the ways to do this is to think from a contingency planning perspective, not succession planning.

Unlike succession planning which focuses on top leaders of the organization, contingency planning focuses on key positions/personnel that affect the daily operation of the business. For instance, assume an organization has one payroll specialist responsible for paying every employee in the organization and there is no one else who can perform this duty. If this payroll specialist leaves the organization for any reason and the organization does not have a backup for this person, employees would not be paid, at least not in a timely manner. Of course, this is only one example. I am certain there are many more examples in which organizations rely on specialized individuals but have no contingency plan for their absence.

Contingency plans for critical positions are not a new idea. In fact, it is an old idea that many businesses have practiced in the past in order to continue their normal business practices. To develop a basic contingency plan for such critical roles, here are a few recommendations:

- Identify key positions/personnel with specialized skills that affect daily operations. To determine whether such positions affect daily operations, utilize the "but for test." But for this role/position, daily operations would stop until replaced by another. If its determined operations stop until replaced by another, then it is a critical role for the operation of the organization.
- Develop a list of these key positions/roles from every department in the organization.
- Prioritize the key roles from most critical to least critical.
- Develop standby strategies for each position. It can involve cross-training others in the department or hiring additional staff who can perform the same duties. Some organizations will outsource as their backup for specific jobs, but be cautious if you are in a union environment. There are bargaining agreement guidelines which may prohibit outsourcing for union bargaining positions.

Lastly, while contingency planning is important, it is not designed to replace succession planning. Rather, it should be an additional enhancement to the organization's succession plan.

Succession Planning:

As mentioned previously, succession planning is designed to identify future executive leaders to replace the current ones in order to continue the business of the organization. This is mostly because people retire, and business must be maintained for the next generation. The concept of succession planning is straightforward enough, yet in practice, most organizations differ. There have been many articles written on how to and what works best. Many of them are helpful, but always remember, they are written from the viewpoint of the author and his/her experience, as I am doing the same. Therefore, it is a good idea to explore various ideas from different HR professionals.

From my perspective, there are two types of succession plans:

1) The Emergency Succession plan, which is designed to identify a second and third in command during the unexpected absence of a leader, such as CEO, CFO, HR, etc.
2) The traditional Long-Term Succession plan, aimed to identify the next leader of the organization and/or department.

Both can be challenging, yet the emergency succession plan is much easier to accomplish than the long-term succession plan. The board of directors does not need to be involved but should be notified for their peace of mind. Each member of the executive team can assign one or two individuals to be their second and third in command. This can be completed informally, but with proper communication to the employee population of the organization.

On the other hand, long-term succession planning is more challenging, simply because it requires plausible forecast for the future operations of the organization. Under the guidance of the board of directors, and facilitated by the executive of HR, the board of directors (usually selected board members) will assemble with the CEO and the executive team for strategic brainstorming sessions about the future of the organization. In such meetings, they must attempt to determine the likelihood of continuous operations in the future and whether the political climate, economic, and other circumstances may affect the organization.

Assuming the probability of change in the future is likely, the next challenge for the board and the executive team is to identify the right skills, behavior, and qualifications needed for the future. Most likely, it begins with the CEO's successor, followed by the other executive team successors. Once completed, the executive team will evaluate the organization's current talent and ascertain whether there are individuals who can be developed into the executive roles. At times, however, outside talent will be required, and recruitment will generally begin one year before an executive's retirement.

Again, this is one method for succession planning of top leaders. Of course, there are other methods that might be more useful for your organization, but that would depend on the discretion of each organization.

Efficiency Practices:

Throughout the years, operational efficiencies have risen in various industries with the overall objective to reduce waste and improve quality and productivity. One popular principle that derived from Toyota Production Systems is Lean Manufacturing. The concept is designed to eliminate waste, lower production costs, reduce standing inventory, increase labor productivity, and continuous improvement. Such a principle was very successful in various manufacturing businesses. Moreover, because of the success of the lean manufacturing idea, these principles were adopted by other industries such as healthcare. Yes, manufacturing and healthcare operate significantly differently. However, the core principles of lean manufacturing created an efficiency mindset which allowed industries such as healthcare to think beyond their normal operating ways.

Of course, principles like lean manufacturing are designed for operational process efficiencies, yet for human resource processes, one will rarely find a formal system for HR operational efficiencies. Some HR departments that are understaffed and believe they are overworked are always in the get-it-done-now mode or putting-out-fires mode. They haven't the time to slow down enough to develop efficiency strategies. Other departments may be fully staffed, and they might believe their system of operations is adequate, with no intention of completing any annual assessment of their processes. It is true, from my knowledge, there is no formal efficiency principle for human resources, but there are methods of utilizing technology and other resources to improve one or two processes, such as recruitment and/or performance management. Such methods can be very useful to improve a specific process, but obviously, each department must come to their conclusions on any of these methods.

One of the values of lean manufacturing is that it has created a mindset for efficiency to industries other than manufacturing. This mindset is a continuous consciousness to improve processes. Like lean manufacturing, this begins with the notion of creating streamlined methods that eliminate staff time while achieving the objectives of the process.

For the human resources departments, HR management, with the assistance of the HR staff, should prioritize all the critical functions of HR. Thereafter, determine which are the most to the least cumbersome processes. In other words, does each process have many procedural steps to be completed to accomplish its objectives? Subsequently, evaluate the most cumbersome process and ascertain whether such process is truly inefficient.

For instance, if the process appeared to have too many procedural steps, ask yourself whether each step is necessary. If such step(s) can be eliminated, would you be able to meet its objectives? On some occasions, some processes may have many procedural steps, yet each step is necessary to accomplish the process's objectives. Therefore, one can reasonably conclude this process is efficient.

Typically, each HR function has its own process that might require a different approach to efficiency evaluation. Nonetheless, the mindset for continuous improvement must be a priority for HR staff and the employee population of the organization.

Leadership Development:

For some organizations, leadership development is usually discussed during succession planning, and it is typically for the preparation of future leaders of the organization. However, even such organizations have or will discover that leaders are needed at all levels of operation, especially if the organization grows larger. Today, most such organizations have embraced leadership development for all levels of management positions, starting with supervisors and ending with executives.

Great leaders are needed at all levels to assist the organization with meeting its objectives. Clearly, good leaders have many benefits. They empower staff and build teamwork, retain good staff, increase productivity, ensure the organization's current and future goals are met, make rational decisions, hold themselves accountable, and teach and develop others.

However, the process of leadership development is not as simple as it seems. Throughout time, some organizations discovered challenges at all levels of leadership development, especially at the supervisory level. For instance, if one is currently a supervisor or manager and is being developed for a higher-level leadership role, the process is simpler than staff-to-supervisor development, since such supervisor or manager has previous training and experience managing staff and is accustomed to more responsibility and accountability.

Staff-to-supervisor training and development is not only very challenging, but some might argue most important. It is a critical stage of development. If it is accomplished with minimal effort (half backed) by the leadership, then the results are less favorable for both the staff and the organization, not to mention the challenges in the future to correct or improve this supervisor. On the other hand, when training is accomplished with utmost effort, the outcome is an excellent supervisor and future upper management professional for the organization.

As organizations become more committed and invested in leadership development, they must determine their current and future needs and how such needs fit with developing leadership for their organization. Even as such organizations grow, change, or turn over leadership, these are the times to evaluate their current and future needs and determine actions. For instance, if a manager decides to leave the organization for another, and such position becomes vacant, the organization must decide whether to replace it, eliminate it, or restructure the position with different duties and responsibilities. If restructuring the position is decided, then the technical skills and behavior attributes must be detailed in the new job description and recruitment ads.

In general, leadership developments require strategic planning for all levels of management positions, from supervisor to executive level. Fundamentally speaking, all levels of leadership (supervisors to executives) share four (4) core foundations that all must possess (which is addressed in detail in the next chapter), though with different degrees of responsibility, accountability, risk, and decision making. The strategic plan should include, but not be limited, to the following:

- Determine current and future management needs for each department; for example, the number of supervisors, managers, directors, etc.
- Determine the skills and behavior necessary for each managerial classification position.
- Modify or create new job descriptions (if necessary) to align such skills and behavior with the organization's needs.
- Since each department has its own discipline, determine the technical skills training needed for each classification.
- Prioritize trainings from most critical to least critical for your organization, whether it be technical skills or human skills, etc.
- Create an organization-wide training calendar which covers the most critical training to the least critical.

- *Most important, determine training methods, whether they be online, classroom setting, in-house training by key staff members, firms specializing in leadership training (vendors), or all the above. However, if you choose vendors to conduct the training, be sure to select the appropriate training modules needed for the staff trainees and the organization.*
- Lastly, begin to facilitate training sessions, but be sure to survey the trainees for the quality of each session.

In the next chapter, I will introduce the Four Fundamental Approach (FFA) to designing leadership training. It is a guideline for creating an infrastructure for leadership training for all levels of management in order to develop balanced leaders from ground zero.

Chapter 4

I. The Four Fundamental Approach (FFA) to Designing Leadership Training

Human Skills	Technical Skills	Business Attributes	Ethical Practices

Leadership is not only having the vision, but also the courage, the discipline, and the resources to get you there.
   —George Washington

I suppose leadership, at one time, meant muscles; but today, it means getting along with people
   —Mahatma Gandhi

When we think of great leaders, we always think of those who have impacted history and humanity the most. In our modern world, leaders come from all facets: athletics, political, educational, business, and many more. The common theme is to influence and lead others to better places and better situations. In the business environment, leaders must have the same leadership characteristics as others, albeit with different responsibilities such as managing their staff to be productive in order to meet organization's objectives. They must develop, train, reward, discipline (if necessary) while creating a great and safe work environment.

In this chapter, I will present a different viewpoint and approach to leadership development. My focus will be on four broad categories and their core elements to be utilized as a foundation for creating a curriculum for a well-rounded leader. First, to set the stage, here is a little background.

For years working as a human resource professional in various industries, I had the opportunity to work with great leaders and significantly terrible ones. I observed many styles of leadership from frontline supervisors to executive level. Many of them share different, yet at times, similar pitfalls, such as…

- Being too commanding or too lenient.
- Lacking clear communication, or too much communicating which confuses others.
- Making frivolous promises and not taking any responsibility for such promises or statements.
- Lack of understanding of staff's jobs or positions.
- Lack of basic business and financial knowledge, in addition to lack of knowledge of company's overall basic operations.
- Unable to create teamwork environment in the department or company.
- Practicing favoritism to certain staff members, and above all, unable to retain great employees.

Such issues have been around for years at all levels of leadership, and year after year, business organizations spend significant amounts of money on supervisory, management, and executive leadership training. While all three levels of leadership have a common goal, which is to lead teams to be more productive and efficient, they are different from the levels of the operations of the business. Normally, supervisors lead frontline staff. Managers lead supervisors and their frontline staff, while executive leaders are heads of the department or organization. Larger organizations have more complex its leadership structure.

As organizations retain firms/companies specializing in leadership training (from novice to seasoned leaders), businesses face three main challenges:

1) A large menu of training topics to choose from.
2) Allocating consistent time to conduct the training.
3) The cost, which can be in the thousands, especially if the business does not have a clear vision of how their leaders should be developed.

Most companies have a few thoughts on what makes a good manager or leader (within the limits of their organization), but rarely do they have an exact idea, and more importantly, the exact foundational elements of leadership in the business world. As with many things in life, *foundations are most important because it's the key to building. It is the underlying principle of ideas,* yet in most cases, foundations are an afterthought, ignored and/or presumed to have already been developed at some point in time.

Throughout those years in HR, I spent a considerable amount of time working with leadership training firms, and I had the opportunity to select exact topics which I believed would best serve those upcoming and current managers/leaders. On one occasion, I selected the training firm's A-to-Z management training program, which should have covered management development from the beginning to advanced stages. Unfortunately, after completion of the training, most found pieces of the training helpful, while others found it to be somewhat confusing. The main reason is that some could not conceive these leadership concepts in practice, especially current or long-time managers.

However, one has to understand how these current or long-term leaders became managers. Many of them had been managing for years and became managers because they had been with the company for a long time, or had advanced technical knowledge of the job, so they'd been promoted by default, as some might say. Unfortunately, while these managers are technically skilled, most were unable to teach, empower, and/or build a teamwork environment. Regrettably, this is a common theme among many organizations and in many industries, including government.

During the time when I chose the A-to-Z training program of one of the best training companies, I sat in and observed every training session, and at the time, I thought the presenter was clear and concise; the material was very detailed and comprised of relevant management/leadership topics. However, after each session, I informally surveyed the manager trainees and asked their honest feedback. Most had positive comments about each session, yet after the completion of the entire training session, many failed to see how it all "fits in the big picture."

Management training firms focus on leadership behavior, of what some would call soft skills, from proper communication to motivating others, but they do not cover other management skills, such as technical skills and business attributes. It is presumed most organizations provide such training for their managers, or such managers were previously trained in these areas. However, as I look back at my experience in the industries of manufacturing and healthcare, I do recall some job training provided for managers, but it lacked consistency with any formal training programs, because of budgetary issues.

What makes a good manager/leader for business operations? What does it take to lead and/or manage people in the work environment? What is the core knowledge that managers must possess to be an efficient leader?

If you look at a typical job description of a manager (regardless of industry), you will see a long list of "Must Know, Must Have, Must Do, and Must Be". It is usually because the organizations who wrote such job descriptions know that it takes more than job skills and delegating duties to be an effective manager. It takes a good understanding of *human behavior*, the *technical skills* for the job, *business attributes*, and *ethical management conduct.* Thus, based on these four broad fundamental categories, I would recommend a different approach for leadership training that organizations can personalize to their culture: 1) it would cover each broad category, 2) the necessary skill elements of each category, and 3) the reasons behind such categories.

II. Human Skills

If you ask most professionals today to describe, in one word, the most important management skills, or what makes a great manager/leader, overwhelmingly, you may find the answer is people skills. In other words, it's the basic human ability to interact with others. It sounds simple enough, yet many managers fail at it for various reasons. Certainly, there are many pitfalls managers should avoid, and while I will mention a few in our discussions, I will focus on the important fundamental human skills managers must have, which hopefully would eliminate and/or avoid any pitfalls which typically occur with less experienced leaders. (For our purposes, "pitfall" is defined as an unforeseen mistake.)

Credibility: The heart of leadership is the ability to influence in order to properly lead others, and that requires strong credibility. Credibility is not a mere *concept* which others discuss, but rather an everyday *conduct* that must be practiced daily. However, establishing credibility is no easy task. Credibility is truthfulness in all areas of leadership, from knowledge of the profession to ethical behavior. To establish credibility takes some steps, and for our management training, it starts with communication.

Communication: *Before you speak, listen. Before you write, think.*
 —***William Shakespeare***

One can spend a significant amount of time focusing on communication training, and many organizations have, yet for our purpose, I want to focus on a few basic communication skills which I believe have been lost throughout time.

What is communication? It is a mutual exchange of ideas between two or more people. It takes listing and speaking, and in today's modern times of emails and other means of communication, it takes reading and writing. Of course, it's not as easy as it sounds. If properly executed, a leader can achieve many objectives, but if poorly executed, it can lead to many problems which would result in defeating organizational objectives.

<u>Listening:</u> You have heard the cliché, "You might be listening but you're not hearing." Well, this statement has some validity. Many of the issues arise out of employee relations, labor relations, and other conflicts in this world because individuals are talking to each other, yet no one is listening to any of the conversation. Yes, we have all been there with family arguments and other, in which arguments escalate to yelling because no one is listening to each other, only talking loudly at each other. Of course, since we are human beings, this happens in the workplace regularly at all levels, from executive to regular staff.

For leaders, lack of listening can be very detrimental simply because if he/she is not listing to others, their leadership credibility will be jeopardized, and of course, especially for new leaders who are trying to develop credibility.

Creating training in the area of Active Listening requires several elements.

- Developing Patience,
- Learning to Identify Relevant and Substantive Facts,
- Ability to Ask Relevant Questions, and
- Ability to Summarize Relevant facts.

Let's take a look a common and vague scenario in the workplace which occurs regularly: An emotional employee comes to you for a problem. That employee cannot adequately express their issue clearly, and in fact, he/she is drifting from one potential problem to another. It is your job to determine the real issues and the severity of each one.

Learning to be an Active Listener allows a manager to identify real issues and properly plan and execute resolutions. Of course, there are many more benefits to being an active listener, for the professional, personal, and social life.

<u>Verbal Communication:</u> This is simply the ability to utilize words in order to convey a message(s). However, it is not as simple as it sounds. For managers or other types of leaders, excellent verbal communications can go a long way, yet poor verbal communications have short and long-term detriments.

Essentially, management training must include ways to develop articulation. To do so, here are some basic criteria:

1) Practice verbalizing complete sentences with proper grammar and without jargon.
2) Practice pronouncing difficult words which will clarify communication more, allow easier pronunciation of simpler words.
3) Develop methods to control emotions, utilizing a monotonic (continuing sound with an unchanging pitch) voice. This is especially helpful during any conflict resolution, negotiations, or other matters that can raise emotions. On many occasions, if a person uses a loud voice and appears aggressive, it can be construed as lacking in confidence. This is a pitfall many leaders fall into subconsciously.
4) On the subject of voice tone, it is not <u>what</u> you say, but <u>how</u> you say it. There will be many times when managers must have a tough conversation with their staff member(s), and it might be a sensitive

topic, embarrassing situation, or disciplinary proceedings.

Diplomatic skills are critical with all tough situations and yet beneficial in other circumstances. One of the most important diplomatic skills is practicing good Etiquette, such as greeting individuals, allowing others to speak without interrupting them, and acknowledging them.

<u>Ability to Influence:</u> Great communication can be gauged by how well someone connects with others and sways them with his/her message. To be influential is the highest standard of communication excellence, and one of the most significant parts of being credible.

Influential people tend to be strong leaders, even if they are not in leadership roles. They can be everyday people working in various jobs but have the courage to speak and touch others. However, being influential can be a double-edged sword. You can inspire and empower others to do great things, or you can lead them on a path of destruction. History has many examples of both. Being influential is a powerful device, and for our purpose, we will be focusing on instrumentally helping others.

There are those who say that you cannot teach others to be influential. I strongly disagree, which is why I believe it should be included in all leadership training. Let's start with what we have already discussed, which is listening and verbal communication.

Once training has been completed in this area, we can focus on the Ability to Influence preparations.

1) Avoiding the sizable pitfall of Making Frivolous Promises. Leaders in all areas, political, business, and/or others, have made frivolous promises which damaged their credibility.

Here is a common scenario. Politicians promise results in a certain amount of time, and they fail their promissory obligations, but the most common is in the workforce environment. When leaders promise their staff and/or others in leadership to take action upon something (whether it be salary increases, program implementations, or change), and he/she does not deliver because of unforeseen events, even though he/she had intended to do so, his/her credibility will have a temporary blemish, which could lead to permanent damage. Ideally, even if one is sure they can deliver on a promise, he/she should always indicate that they will "try" to do their best to accomplish such tasks. Do not make definitive promises. People understand the challenges that come from change, but one thing they do not want to hear is "lip service" which is basically frivolous promises.

2) Building Relations or Connecting with Others. There are many trainings have been developed in this area, and most of them are very good.

However, the most important training guide I will emphasize is about the First Contact with others.

The first contact sets the atmosphere for communication (whether it be positive or negative) and sets the stage for the relationship. There are a few pitfalls one should avoid during first contact:

- a) Do not make personal judgment of the person's appearance, racial, style, age, or any other. Yes, that's easier said than done, but imagine yourself stuck in the elevator or somewhere else with a person different than you. Most likely, you or the other person will begin a conversation, and in a short time, you will discover many things you both might have in common. As a result, you both made a connection.
- b) Be humble during first contact, because nothing shows a lack of confidence and alienating others when one is not humble, especially during first contact.
- c) Most importantly, practice empathy. In other words, put yourself in the other person's place, and imagine how he/she feels.

d) Find some common ground with another because every human being has things in common, it is a matter of discovering it.

3) Being Prepared: Generally speaking, most professionals prepare themselves for any business meetings, whether to present or give feedback on topics. There is another preparation that many rarely practice, and it is Anticipatory Preparations.

Anticipatory preparation is simply anticipating other topics or issues presented, or in some cases, anticipating rebuttals and/or questions to presented topics. During negotiations, it can also be used to anticipate the desires and the opposing opinions of the other party. For us, the importance of anticipation is to illustrate overall knowledge, as well as to be in stronger position during any negotiations. That said, preparing to anticipate takes the practice of Empathy, the Ability to think about all sides of the topic or issue, and Argue and Question all sides of the topic and issue.

<u>Written Communication:</u> Too many misunderstandings occur from unclear emails, texts, company ads, public statements, and more. With today's social media use (both for business and private), writing has become fast food. Unfortunately, some professionals have carried that cavalier writing to their professional emails, and it should not be acceptable.

In this area, training should be focused on the following:

a) Basic email etiquette: always starting emails with a greeting and ending with a customary "thank you, best regards" and other professional goodbyes. Additionally, do not use popular jargon in your greetings and goodbyes, such as Ciao, Cheers, and others. That lacks professionalism.
b) While drafting an email or responding to an email, use simple sentence structure, with proper grammar and proper spelling, and do not forget to read your draft before sending.
c) Keep it as concise as possible. Every paragraph in a professional email should have substance, and anything that appears to be conversational should be eliminated. {One caveat: There will be times when conversational emails are acceptable with others, but one must be able to distinguish the difference between the two and not mistakenly converse in professional emails.}

Resolving Conflicts:

In a workplace environment, conflicts among staff and/or management occur regularly and randomly. Unfortunately, it happens for many reasons, and usually, if problems escalate, it can lead to long-term damage for both the organization and staff.

Typically, the process of conflict resolution is managed by those professionals in the human resources department, so why must managers learn to resolve conflicts? Managers work directly with their staff and have the opportunity to resolve any issue swiftly before it escalates to bigger problems. In addition, managers are leaders of their staff and the staff will constantly look for guidance from their leader.

Of course, it would only be reasonable for leaders to grasp the basic process of conflict resolution. Ideally, it is best to identify potential conflict and take some action to avoid escalation. Like many problems, conflicts have symptoms, and like medical science, these symptoms are an indication of abnormalities.

<u>Symptoms of potential conflict:</u> Developing a guideline to identify prospective conflicts can avoid actual conflicts, but be cautious of reading too much into something and taking action with few facts. That can be very damaging as well.

For example, if two people have a debate or have disagreements during work, it may not be cause for alarm unless both parties stop communicating to each other more than three days, or the debate continues in an unfriendly manner. In this situation, intervention is necessary before it escalates. There are signs to look for potential conflicts and the list can be large. However, in general, discontented, disconnected, and disengaged are elements of potential conflicts.

<u>Clash of the Titans:</u> A conflict has risen between two strong-headed, well-established professionals on the same work team. Their manager must attempt to resolve these issues before escalation. Training in the Process of Conflict Resolution should be as follows:

1) Meet with each party separately and obtain all the facts which led the dispute. However, take into account that each party might be emotional and may make random and personal statements not relevant to the actual dispute. In this situation, listening for the relevant facts and repeating those facts to the staff members will help clarify the actual issue(s) that are being disputed.
2) Ask each of the disputing parties to describe their ideal resolution or outcome. This tactic will show the intent of the parties, eliminating any guessing of each party's expectation. It will also show how reasonable or unreasonable each party might be in this dispute. There are times in which each party will ask for the most, and on certain occasions, it may be unreasonable, which will lead us to the next step.

3) This step might a little more challenging because a manager has to find common objectives among the parties in order to have a mutual understanding. One widely used tactic is to negotiate a compromise with each party separately and come to a final agreement. This may require back-and-forth discussions with all parties until an agreement is met. [Note: An important element to remember is to check organization's policies (if any) on the disputed issue(s). It's likely it will assist or guide with any resolutions.]

<u>Ability to Negotiate:</u> Training managers to negotiate is vital for their ability to excel in their careers. There might be times when managers will be "on the table" during union contract or other contract negotiations, or even perhaps representing their organization with purchasing and selling materials. Negotiate skills have many benefits, which include but are not limited to the ability to use Reasoning and Compromise in all areas of management.

What is negotiation? Simply, it is communication between two or more people in order to arrive to an agreement(s). It requires Patience, Empathy, Diplomacy, Courage, and Emotional Control.

Developing negotiation training should be focused on the following:

a) How to negotiate (i.e., Negotiations 101).
b) Practicing with different scenarios, both verbal and/or written. For example, developing hypothetical situations in which the trainees can either write or verbalize their approach, their tactics, and their solutions for the facts presented. (Important note: By challenging trainees to find their own tactics and solutions, it would empower them to be creative and assist with building confidence).
c) Setting Reasonable Expectations for the outcome of an agreement. Strategic negotiators plan negotiation tactics before any meeting, and usually, they will have a long list of wants. However, these negotiators will also set priorities as to the most important wants to the least. They know they will not achieve every task on that list, but hopefully the most important ones. Negotiations is about everyone (on both sides) gaining some and giving up some. It is the ultimate compromise, which is why setting reasonable expectations allows for positive outcomes for everyone.

Creating a Teamwork Environment:

By now, the concept of teamwork is widely accepted among most, if not all organizations. Certainly, there have been many good and different approaches to teamwork through publications and trainings. What makes the teamwork environment vital to organizations? Well, if you examine the typical organization, it is made up of people with special skills and functions that contribute to the goals and mission of the organization. Of course, the challenge will always fall on organizational leaders and their managers to align those skills and functions to meet the goals of the organization and fulfill its mission.

As manager of a department or a team, her/his job is to assure their staff's work is being completed in a timely manner. Again, the completed work will further the goals and the mission of the organization while maintaining positive morale among the staff. In doing so, there are some criteria managers must learn, if not strengthen, in order to create a teamwork environment.

- Motivation and motivation tactics
- Empowerment
- Developing staff
- Identifying talent

<u>Motivation:</u> The most effective element of the human mind is being motivated to achieve, and it is, perhaps, the most difficult to obtain. It creates a desire to do something or behave a certain way, but unfortunately, the challenge has always been maintaining motivation for lengthy periods of time.

In the work environment, it is the manager's job to motivate others on his/her staff, but before doing so, managers must evaluate their staff before committing to a plan. First, let us examine the people in the workforce. Typically, there are four types:

1) The self-motivated person who is driven by goal accomplishment and may only need expectations set or perhaps direction.
2) The middle-of-the-road person who is there to put in his/her time and usually meet the job requirements.
3) The person barely meeting expectations but is trying hard to do so.
4) The person who has the skills but is not meeting any expectations or trying to do so.

<u>Motivation Theories:</u> There are many theories on how to motivate individuals for many different challenges in life, but in the workplace, there are limitations simply because there is only one challenge: to motivate others to do their job well.

In the past, leaders used strong tactics, like the <u>Military Drill Sergeant approach,</u> in which they display extreme dissatisfaction with their employee's work by overly critiquing projects and other work-related matters. However, if employees exceed their boss's expectations, that boss might give some positive feedback on their work product. The theory behind this tactic is to use more negativity and harshness to bring out the best in people. In certain circumstances, it works. We have often seen human beings endure tough challenges and overcame it, and in time, surpassed it. The problem with this approach is it does not work with every personality in the workforce. It only works on those who are very resilient, but even with those individuals, there might be negative long-term impact, such as burnout, unappreciated feelings, lack of security, and more. I consider this approach a pitfall and discourage those leaders from practicing it.

Another, more commonly used concept (past and present) is <u>Reinforcement and Punishment.</u> It was first introduced by the behavioral psychologist, B. F. Skinner. It is a straightforward concept because it acknowledges the most primal basic human behavior, which is pleasure and pain. This school of psychology maintains that behavior is determined by its consequences, whether it be reinforcement or punishment. This makes it more or less likely that the behavior will occur again. For example, in the workplace, organizations use disciplinary measures to correct behavior or actions which violate their policies while rewarding those which further the organization's goals and sustain its mission.

Although awareness of these concepts is important from a historical and learning perspective, there is more to developing motivational training for employees.

One important note to remember is that motivating a group and motivating an individual takes different strategies and approaches, simply because people tend to behave differently in groups than they do one-on-one.

Group Motivation: Our society has many examples of singular individuals who have the talent for motivating groups of people, from athletic and life coaches to public figures and religious leaders. What do they all have in common? They all have an ability to provide a positive outlook for the future, in other words, hope. However, the difference between those who are successful versus those who are not is the capacity for being genuine.

Secondary Mission and Objectives: Certainly, in a work environment, it is no different. Leaders or team leaders must have a genuine belief in the mission and goals of the organization, must provide a positive outlook for the future of the team and/or department, but above all, team leaders must develop their own goals and subsidiary mission for their team. The purpose of having a subsidiary mission is to be more team and/or department specific, while staying within the overall guidelines of the organizational mission. Once established, Team Leaders must communicate the subsidiary mission and the objectives to the team. (Note: Objectives must have reasonable timelines.)

<u>Establishing Team Reward(s):</u> Establishing rewards for a team can be a very subjective process. Each organization has its own culture and will view rewards differently. In the United States, incentives and rewards are part of the culture, and it would only stand to reason that many American organizations would adopt these values. There are those organizations that may see things differently. While many argue people need incentives to perform at higher level, others may argue it is about work ethics, which means those with strong work ethics will perform without expectation of reward, while those with weaker work ethics might need incentives to perform better.

Team leaders must consider the following before implementing team rewards:

1) The culture of the organization and whether this practice is acceptable.
2) If acceptable, consider long-term and short-term rewards. (An example of long-term rewards is for the employee to be part of a great and accomplished team that he/she can utilize to further their

career. A short-term reward would be a monetary bonus or a few more vacation days.)
3) Be creative with any rewards and attempt to survey staff as to whether they would like such rewards.

Maintaining Motivation:

Once Team Leaders establish motivation for the team, the challenge becomes one of maintaining this motivation throughout months. Like rewards, there are many ways of doing so, and it takes creativity. However, Team Leaders must be cognitive of maintaining motivation with the team. One tactic is to reinforce the goals and the mission of the team and/or department every few months during staff meetings and encourage open conversation as to the challenges and/or successes of work projects.

Celebrating Small Successes:

As Team Leaders monitor their team's progress, they must never forget to celebrate the small successes which moved the goals further. Celebrating small successes is another way of giving positive feedback to the team. An important aspect in this situation is any rewards for small successes should be relatively small, perhaps a special team luncheon or gift cards. The main reason is to maintain balance between the level of success and the level of celebration.

Recognizing:

In Maslow's Hierarchy of Needs, when discussing Esteem needs, Maslow points out the importance for employees to achieve, be respected, and have self-respect in the workplace. Of course, one way to achieve this is being recognized for one's achievements by others, whether by co-workers or a direct supervisor. Recognition is acknowledgment for doing something positive, and in the workplace, it could mean good job performance, good teamwork deeds, and willingness to help others.

Team Leaders must identify all the individuals who are making such successful impact on the team, whether as a group and/or individually. That sounds simple enough, yet unfortunately, for many leaders, this simple concept is difficult to practice for various reasons. For some, they over-analyze and make wrong presumptions as to how to recognize employees, while others do nothing for fear of failure.

To simplify an approach, consider the following:

a) Consistently observe staff for progress.
b) Consistently be conscious of acknowledging staff.
c) Use empathy as much as possible.
d) Thank staff through different means, such as in person, handwritten note, or any other way. Be creative.

Lastly, consider building an Employee Recognition Team, mixed with leaders and staff to create recognition ideas and ways to implement them. One key note: recognition is paramount to building a teamwork environment. In addition, it supports developing individuals with their career path.

Staff Supporting Staff:

There are many ways to gauge whether Team Leaders were successful in creating a teamwork environment, but one stands out more than others, and that is staff supporting other staff/team members with achieving organizational and/or departmental objectives. On some occasions, it happens organically as a result of creating a team environment, but on other occasions, it is encouraged and influenced by Team Leaders. Of course, each Team Leader must find his/her own style of communication and influence to assure staff members supporting each other.

Empowering Individuals:

In recent times, we hear the term empowerment used in the workplace as a motivational tool, management style, and an embraced value, but what does it mean? Why is it an embraced value? Empowerment is simply allowing others to become stronger or more confident by giving them independence to make decisions. It is a welcomed value because it is the opposite of micromanagement.

Micromanagement is a style of management which allows managers to control their staff on all levels, without any room for staff to make any independent decisions. Those who micromanage might argue that, since they are held accountable for their staff's work, they need to make certain things are getting completed properly. However, this practice can be time-consuming and has the tendency to exhaust the manager. In addition, this practice leaves no room for staff to learn, both from mistakes and from accomplishments.

Throughout the years, organizations have discovered micromanagement is detrimental to their organizations, from high turnovers of skilled staff to low morale, which of course, hinders creativity and high performance. In time, most organizations embraced the idea of empowerment, and while many employees have benefited from being empowered to achieve, some, albeit a marginal group, were unaffected by it. (See my previous discussion on the four types of employees.)

Empowering others does not come naturally. There are steps one can learn and practice, and here are few guidelines:

<u>It begins with Trust:</u> In order for staff to feel empowered, they have to believe their Team Leader trusts them. For Team Leaders, sometimes this is a difficult undertaking, since they are held accountable for any mistakes of their staff. However, it must be done.

<u>Challenge staff with responsibilities:</u> Team Leaders should be very mindful of assigned projects. Projects should be reasonably challenging in accordance to each person's core skills but not be overwhelming, setting someone up to fail. *(See later discussion about development.)*

<u>Challenge staff through brainstorming:</u> During staff meetings, leaders should always involve the entire staff, whether they are seasoned professionals or novices, with brainstorming conversations. Basically, brainstorming is a spontaneous group discussion designed to develop new ideas or find answers to challenging questions. In these circumstances, everyone has some valuable thought to offer. While in some circumstances, the novice staff may not participate as much as the seasoned professionals, leaders should give them an opportunity to be heard in another time,

whether in private or staff meetings. Sometimes, great ideas come later, not in the moment.

<u>Set timelines for both projects and review:</u> As Team Leaders assign projects and responsibilities, they must allocate timelines for completion, but more importantly, they must allocate a time for feedback and review. This is crucial to assure the staff is getting the support, feedback, and guidance to succeed.

<u>Learning from failure:</u> No single professional has ever succeeded without many failures. It is simply human. Team Leaders need to emphasize this point to their staff. Team Leaders must turn failure into learning moments. (*See later discussion about development.*)

<u>Recognize their accomplishments:</u> Team Leaders must recognize his/her staff's accomplishments, no matter the size the achievement. Positive reinforcement is a necessary tool for empowerment of staff.

<u>Developing individuals:</u> One of the most critical roles, and some might argue the most difficult, is developing staff, whether for higher and more skilled positions or different positions that require special skill sets. There are many benefits to developing staff, which include but are not limited to talent retention, good morale in the work environment, and contributing to the continuation of the organization's objective and mission. How to begin? Should every staff member be developed?

In theory, every staff member should be developed, unfortunately, not every staff member has the desire to be developed for bigger or different positions. Some staff members are happy where they are, and of course, that is acceptable. As Team Leader, he/she must learn to identify A) those who have the willingness to be developed, B) those individuals who have the core competencies to learn different skills sets, and C) the time commitments for training and so forth.

However, there are those individuals who are **passive** about professional growth, but generally have potential to be developed for more than their current position. Nevertheless, on many occasions, these individuals are overlooked by Team Leaders on the presumption that, since they showed little interest in development, they must be happy in their current position. While this might be the case in certain circumstances, Team Leaders should nonetheless attempt to identify those who have the potential for growth, not only for the benefit of the staff, but for the organization's benefit.

<u>Learning to identify talent:</u> There are trainings in the area of identifying talent or potential talent. They are typically a part of leadership curriculum with many professional leadership trainers. However, there are certain behaviors and practices Team Leaders should know and perform.

1) Always be consciously looking for future talent that can continue and/or elevate the work for the organization. In other words, learn and practice succession planning.
2) Observe a staff member for his/her efforts, quality of work, team behavior, and other skills which might be beneficial for the team and organization.
3) Watch what makes such individuals passionate about their work, or perhaps other passions that could lead to development.

Development stage: Assuming a Team Leader has identified a prospective talent to be developed, now the challenge is where to start? It begins with the vision and a goal.

The Vision: is the end result expected from the development stage. The staff member and Team Leaders both have a vision of what they hope to gain after this development stage.

The Goal(s): are set by the Team Leader, with regularly scheduled follow-up meetings to monitor progress, engage in discussion, and assist with any challenges. In addition, such progress meetings must have timelines, from when it begins to a tentative completion date. {Important Note: Team Leaders must set reasonable, challenging goals which can be achieved with resilient effort but avoid setting high goals that are impossible to achieve. Create a standard for goal setting which can be applied to others in this position in order to ensure fairness and uniformity.}

<u>Progress Meeting:</u> As mentioned, progress meetings must have a timeline, from the first stage of development to the last stage of accomplishment. Assuming the Team Leader and his/her staff have set a reasonable goal for development, thereafter, the Team Leader will be responsible for creating or obtaining the teaching method for development, which will include the subject matter curriculum.

The subjects in the curriculum can be used to assist with creating the progress meeting agenda. For example, the first topic on the curriculum that the staff member completes should be one of the topics to discuss in the first meeting. In these situations, Team Leader must reinforce, help explain, and on some occasions, teach. However, if the subject matter is very technical, and is not within the expertise of the Team Leader, Team Leader must have the staff member explain what he/she has learned. This not only reinforces the training, but also, if they can explain it, then they have learned it.

<u>Challenging and Teaching moments:</u> There is no doubt there will be challenges, failures, and at times, things do not go smoothly. This is a crucial time for Team Leaders to engage the staff member during this process and turn every mistake, challenge, or failure into teaching

moments. Teaching moments are simply those times when you look at failures and mistakes and learn something from them, whether to evaluate and/or change the initial approach or to avoid repeating an action. Either way, this is truly the most educational period of any stage of development.

Expectation: As previously mentioned in the goal setting stage, both Team Leader and staff must have reasonable expectations of the outcome of the development. I emphasize "reasonable" simply because there are times, when both parties may not be 100% satisfied with the outcome of the development, yet to avoid negative feelings and reactions, both parties must look at the positive outcomes, and learn from the negative ones. On most occasions, the development phase is positive for all parties, and as it should be. The staff member will gain knowledge and further his/her career objectives, while the Team Leader gains personal and professional gratification. Of course, the organization will benefit the most simply because they would increase their staff's talent and further the mission and objectives of the organization.

Conclusion: By understanding and practicing the human skills of managing people, the resulting benefits are infinite for the staff and the organization, yet for the leader, it is one quarterly portion of establishing complete credibility.

III. Technical Proficiencies/Specialized Skills

Unlike public officials, leaders in the workforce are required to have certain technical proficiencies to lead others in the organization, department, and/or teams. These technical proficiencies are necessary to ensure the assigned job(s) are completed properly, but also, it ensures leaders can teach and develop others in the team and/or organization.

What are technical proficiencies? Generally speaking, technical proficiencies are specialized skills and understanding of how a particular professional job functions and its responsibilities. For example, a technically proficient person can be anything from a doctor to an electrician, yet the one thing they all share in common is, at some point, they received formal education by achieving a degree and/or certification. Of course, there are others who obtained their professional skills through job experience and training, and while they may not have certifications, most would still consider them technically proficient.

Why do leaders need technical skills? For one, leaders need to make decisions, and at times, they need to make tough decisions on challenging situations in the area of specialty.

Lack of overall technical knowledge may lead to bad decisions, which likely could be detrimental to the department and/or organization.

Perhaps such leaders want to improve processes, and if they lack technical skills, they will most likely fail. Of course, not having any of those specialized skills will eventually lead to improper decisions, which in the long term, can impact the department and/or organization negatively.

<u>Improving technical skills for leadership:</u> As time goes by, most leaders become too busy and, on many occasions, overwhelmed with daily, weekly, and monthly work challenges. The thought of improving or even refreshing one's technical skills never seems to be necessary for leaders, partly because of the mindset of "been there, done that," which means they have obtained their knowledge in the past and feel no need to repeat it. Unfortunately, what most leaders do not realize is, if you are not using some or all the technical skills regularly, one will forget some elements of such skills, and many times, those elements are critical.

I would agree when one has completed a full course in a particular subject matter, he/she does not have to repeat the entire course to refresh or improve one's skills.

In fact, there are several tactics to refreshing and improving skills:

- Going back to your notes or past textbooks and find key areas might need refreshing, of course, if past notes and text books still exist.
- Seminars or Webinars on key topics that are designed to update once current knowledge of certain topics.
- Utilize publication from technical professional sites.
- Utilize or develop a network of professionals and exchange in discussion about topics relating to technical skills and perhaps tactics.
- Finally, RESEARCH. This is my favorite category, but the difficult part of research is completing a self-analysis and identifying those skills that needs refreshed or improved.

Develop a method to teach/train others by developing a training manual.

Not all leaders can teach. In fact, some will argue that most leaders are incapable of teaching or training others for many reasons. The most obvious reason is they do not know how. The other reason is time, simply because most leaders' time is consumed with the daily challenges of their department and/or organization. Unfortunately, because good leaders are in high demand in most industries, this is one criterion rarely sought after during the hiring process.

One solution for leaders is to develop or learn to develop training manuals for different technical skill. The purpose of the training manual is to ensure consistencies with training and practice. Training manuals are a technical document designed to communicate a standard of practice to be used for the training for consistent workflow. Most department heads or managers of operations rely heavily on such documents, not only to ensure consistencies, but to avoid recreating operational training time after time.

How to develop training manuals:

There are many guides and tools on the web which can help with developing training manuals, including books and articles, and they can all be helpful. However, before beginning to draft a training manual, assess the training needs and identify the areas, subject matter, or work processes in which training is critical. Subsequently, develop a general timeline, and utilize change management strategies. In addition, utilize any tool that might be helpful, whether software, handouts, outlines, presentation boards, etc. Thereafter, begin outlining the training subject(s) or process from where it begins to where it should end. Once completed, the outline will be used as the table of contents for the training manual.

Outline sample:

- Introducing the training process/topic and set result expectations after completing the training,
- Define and detail the purpose of the training topic or process,
- Begin with the first stage of training, which is the start of the topic or process,
- Continue to the central part of the training (it should be detailed in the outline),
- Conclude with the last stage of the training (it should be detailed in the outline).

Develop refreshing training summaries:

Once the training manual is completed, begin to develop summaries of each training subject matter. Essentially, the summaries are general key areas of that subject highlighted, without the details, in the actual training manual. It is designed to be used a tool to refresh the training without completing the entire training from the beginning. Typically, the refresher summaries should be about a page or two which can be handed to individuals or of course have available electronically.

The main challenge with the summaries is NOT to recreate the training manual by over-writing, but rather prioritizing the subjects and summarizing in an easy outline format. One thought is to use the table of contents of the original training manual as an outline. Thereafter, utilize the key topics and write a brief training refresher. Of course, there is no standard for writing summaries for training, so one can be as creative in various ways.

IV. Business Attributes Skills

One of the most critical pitfalls of leaders in any stage of their career is the inability to think organizationally. What that means is, typically, such leaders tend to focus on their departmental or team needs without considering the needs of other departments. Because of this, actions taken by such leaders can, and eventually will, have a negative impact on other departments, which will ultimately hurt the organization.

Let's assume there is an organization with leaders who lack such organizational thinking, but it is not evident? How does one determine if such leaders are not thinking organizationally?

One way is to look at the overall operations and determine whether the infrastructure is operationally adequate. Is the daily workflow streamlined and efficient without individuals making exception or continuously modifying processes to fulfill the objectives? Do departmental leaders share best practices and collaborate with each other? Is there a culture of criticizing or complimenting other leaders?

Some might say there is a little of everything, some lack of efficiency, some collaboration, some criticize while others might compliment, and of course, this is true for many organizations.

Ideally, however, the objective ratio should always be more collaboration, less criticism, and much more praise and positive feedback than the contrary.

Industry Knowledge:

Part of thinking organizationally is to understand the business industry in which one is employed, whether high-tech, healthcare, manufacturing, etc. Each industry has a unique culture and industry standard for conducting business, and for leaders, it is vital to understand the purpose of the business and how it operates, especially from revenue generating aspect.

True, there are many facets to business, and having in depth knowledge in all the areas of business might be impossible, however, having general knowledge in most areas of business is conceivable and very helpful.

The benefits of such allow leaders a macro view of business operations. Essentially, it should show how organizational departments work with synchronicity in order to be effective and efficient. This should also trigger the notion of teamwork and working together proficiently. Unfortunately, while this seems obvious, in some if not most cases, departmental leaders and their staff do not synchronize their goals and efforts with other departments, which is one of the reasons for most internal conflicts.

Thus, how do you develop basic organizational skills without pursuing a degree in business? Imagine you've been hired as a new manager for an industry in which you had little exposure from past experience, and now you must understand the fundamentals of this business. Well, you start by the following examination:

- Examine the Purpose of the business.
- Who are the clients/customers of the business?
- How does this organization produce revenue? From customers only and/or other?
- Who regulates such business entities?
- What culture exists in this organization?

Once you can answer these five questions, you will have a better idea of how this business entity operates from a largescale level.

Basic Budgeting:

One of the most critical responsibilities of all managers is to be financially responsible in all their work activities, from hiring and promoting staff to spending allocations for supplies and other miscellaneous needs. It's critical because if overspending occurs, and it continues to occur, the organization will cease to properly function and ultimately "go out of business." Of course, this is where managing a budget is vital.

What is a budget? In a nutshell, a budget is simply a guideline to keep track of spending allocation within an estimated generated income. In small or large organizations, the finance department works closely with departmental leaders to help create such budget.

However, this is an area in which most new leaders have trouble understanding, especially when first promoted or hired by a new organization and seeing their budget for the first time. A spreadsheet with lots of categories and lots of numbers, and if one is lucky, someone in the finance department can help explain it.

The simplest way to understand budgeting is to understand basic budgeting. For example, I assume and hope everyone reading this has a household budget, in which one does not spend more than one makes, which is the first and most important rule of a budget. In a nutshell, it is that simple: calculate your generated income, all actual expenses (including bills etc.), and create manageable spending that would allow you to save money. At times, you will "break even," but as long as you do not lose money regularly and are able to manage it, you should be fine. Conceptually, a business budget is not much different, but it's a bit more complicated. However, it's easy to learn once you understand the parameters of your organization's budgetary process.

Forecasting:

According to Investopedia.com, "Forecasting is a technique that uses historical data as inputs to make informed estimates that are predictive in determining the direction of future trends." In the business world, forecasting is a tool used to determine allocations for budgets, anticipate expenses for the future, and it is also used to determine the right amount of staff needed for a given workday, etc.

For new and advanced leaders, this tool is necessary to learn and understand. It would enable each leader to manage current tasks and plan future tasks to maintain continuous operations in whatever industry one is in. Because of today's time in which knowledge is at one's fingertips by utilizing the internet, one can effortlessly learn the basics of forecasting in a short time. This knowledge and practice will elevate one's basic business skills.

Change Management:

For most who have never heard of this term, "change management," the term is somewhat confusing. I remember when I first heard of this term when it was introduced to employees in a management meeting. Most of the employees thought it meant changing management personnel. Yes, I was one of those employees. In time, I did understand the term and learned the concept well, and in later years, I began to explain the term to others differently to reflect its concept (i.e. from change management to managing change).

Change management is an orderly process that requires discipline, organizational skills, and above all, good planning. This method has been used in business, but in today's time, many industries have used it to make essential changes in their organization. There are two major popular methods, the John Kotter's "8-Step Change Model," and the Kurt Lewin's "Change Management Model." Conceptually, both methods are similar but their approaches are slightly different. Both were proven to be effective, although most pick the one that suits their style.

In years past, seldom would anyone in leadership think about changing management. In fact, some have seen it as a task for project managers only. Well, that's simply not true. Today, everyone in leadership has to lead some change in their department, team, or tackle new projects. Change management tactics are a great way to be timely organized from start to finish. Of course, Kotter and Lewin's methods are proven to be successful, but if one would like to use them as guideline and create their own process that works best, it is also acceptable, provided it accomplishes the goal.

Time Management:

In any employment environment today, a leader is strained with multiple tasks and projects, and while the notion of being a multitasker was a "good thing" years ago, it only proved to be inefficient and taxing for the individual. I still recall professionals mentioning on their resumés and cover letters that they are an excellent multitasker, which was intended to show they are willing to take on many duties. Unfortunately, many did not realize at the time that multitasking does not work. I once read that the enemy of time management is multitasking, and I absolutely agree with such statement, simply because multitasking disregards thoroughness. Attempting to complete multiple tasks in a short amount of time or at the same time only creates a more likelihood of making mistakes, in some cases, creating miscommunication.

On the other hand, time management is a more thoughtful process. It is the process of organizing and planning how to divide one's time between specific tasks. It is designed to allow others to work efficiently on various projects or daily tasks. Of course, there are several methods that, again, one can find with a little research or a seminar course. However, the one key note to remember is in all time management methods is the ability to distinguish between *important tasks and urgent* tasks. In most work environments, others will always say this project or task is important, yet rarely will anyone will distinguish the difference between the two, important and urgent. This is an important element to remember with any time management process one chooses.

Professional Presentation:

In years past, professional presentation was not only encouraged but required in order to be in any leadership role. Today, there are clear struggles among emerging leaders as to what it takes to have a professional presentation. Is it appearance, communications, conduct, or all? The short answer is yes, all the above: appearance, verbal, non-verbal, written communication, and conduct. Since I covered written and verbal communication in a previous discussion, I will focus on appearance, non-verbal communication, and conduct.

<u>Appearance:</u> I've heard the arguments numerous times that how one dresses is not as important as it should be, and it should not be a factor in the professional workplace. Perfect examples are some of the leaders of the High-Tech world, such as Mark Zuckerberg and the late Steve Jobs, who are consistently in a T-shirt but rarely in a professional suit. Well, certainly there are two schools of thought on this topic. One states as long as leaders have substance, professional attire is irrelevant, while others will argue that professional attire is part of the whole platform

of being professional. The argument will continue and there might be a change in the future, but one thing we know for a fact is there are certain times when professional attire is required, such as in court proceedings, legislative hearings, etc.

Traditionally, it has been established that professional clothing is necessary for one's professional credibility. However, professional clothing does not necessarily mean suits for men and women. It could also be uniforms, such as those worn by Police Officers, Firefighters, Military personnel, or even service professionals like car mechanics. These uniforms are the professional attire which accompanies the specific profession and represent a structured work organization. The public knows, when they see a police officer, they know he/she is a cop.

Similarly, for those leaders who work in a corporate structure (whether for profit or not), professional wear is essential part of their presence, specifically when formally addressing staff or presenting in a public forum. A friend once said a person dressing professionally is one more part of the whole professional package and failing to do so would be cheating oneself.

<u>Nonverbal Communication:</u> This is basically the expression of emotions without the use of words. Typically, it is expressed with one's facial features, such as a smile, which indicates happiness or pleasure, or a frown, which

indicates displeasure of some type, and of course body language, which might indicate many things, but you get the idea.

Most human beings have the tendency to attempt to read others by their body language, especially facial expressions. At times, a person can sit in deep thought without any facial expression, yet you will find others attempting to read this person's thoughts, etc. What this shows is humans are accustomed to nonverbal communication, in spite of any verbal language. In essence, nonverbal communication is universal throughout every country and culture.

For leaders, it is important to be very conscious of one's body language and facial expression at all times. For example, having an important conversation with a staff member or a colleague with a "what the hell are you talking about" look is disrespectful, and in most cases, is unnecessary. Sitting or standing in an awkward way might make someone feel uncomfortable. Remember, the professional environment is not intended to be as comfortable as one's home or their favorite hangout.

Professional presence is a vital part of their overall leadership credibility. All professional leaders must make nonverbal communication intentional rather than reactive. He/she must show concern, empathy, disagreement, agreement, or other when the occasion calls for it, but again, without overreacting. While some might think overreaction is a good sign of someone caring, to many others, it shows a lack of emotional control and discipline. As we are all humans, at times, overreaction will occur. Nonetheless, as professionals, being conscious and intentional of nonverbal communication will reduce overreaction. Some might not be aware that overreaction by one (verbal or nonverbal) can disrupt good communication, and it might be difficult to recover from it in a short or long time.

How should leaders be trained on topic? *First, the training must be included in any leadership training. Second, have a list of "do and don't," and third, practice with different scenarios. Completion of this training will result in nonverbal consciousness and awareness of one's surroundings in the professional environment.*

V. Ethics, Practice & Conduct

It is rare to find the subject of ethics in leadership training today. In fact, like technical skills, most professional leadership trainers presume that organizations have addressed or trained on these topics at some point in the tenure of any leader. However, when it comes to ethics, most organizations treat it as a policy, whether in the board bylaws, compliance, or workforce policies. While it is important to have ethics policies in these areas, it is more important to put ethics to practice. What defines ethics? Why is it necessary to include in leadership training? In what areas is ethics practical and relevant?

Generally speaking, ethics can be defined as a set of moral principles that defines good and bad behavior as it applies to society as a whole. The last few decades have given rise to scandals, corruption, and mistreatment of others, and the need to implement and enforce ethical conduct in the workplace has become paramount. However, many of the ethical enforcement has been in a form of staff disciplinary actions, such as termination, suspension, or other, and even with such action, many have criticized the process as being inconsistent and unfair. This is partly because most staff members receive an ethics policy during their new hire and are asked to read and sign it, acknowledging that they will follow such policy.

In most cases, people are ethical in the workplace, but at times, certain negative emotions occur during stressful circumstances, and some people might unintentionally react abnormally and wrongfully. Such reaction can be toward a colleague, subordinate staff, or other members of the organization. Obviously, this is not good behavior or productive toward any organizational goals, yet unfortunately, it does happen, and it will happen again in certain occasions, unless the organization incorporates ethics training as part of their leadership training curriculum.

Creating Ethical Training:

As a general rule, organizations should have ethics training as part of their overall compliance, which tends to cover financial responsibilities, mandatory reporting, and "whistle blower" reporting and protection from retaliation. However, for personnel matters, organizations usually will refer to human resources, and most likely, there are workforce policies that address certain bad behavior or professional conduct responsibilities. However, for leaders, accountability is much higher than it is for ordinary staff, which is even more reason for emphasizing ethical conduct while managing employees and in general interactions.

Should organizations have additional ethics training for leaders? The simple answer is yes. As you will discover in our discussion, ethical conduct applies to all personnel functions in various ways, and the purpose of creating additional training is to generate awareness in such functions. Next, I will focus on several categories of HR functions and the important reasons such categories require ethics training.

Performance Appraisals or Reviews:

One can argue that the most controversial process is Performance Appraisals or Performance Reviews. It is controversial because it is one of the most debated processes in business, as to whether it is necessary to have or not. Other issues arising from performance reviews include the dissatisfaction of employees, even when individuals receive a positive review. However, from an ethical standpoint, many employees, including management staff, have been the subject of bias and wrongful performance review outcomes, in which their direct supervisor has unjustifiably given a bad performance evaluation, made inappropriate comments in this process, and/or set unreasonable performance expectations knowing the employee cannot achieve it. Typically, the motivation behind this might be to demote from one's current position, hold back promotions, or terminate such employees for whatever personal reason(s) of that supervisor.

Like many unethical conducts, the ramifications are predictable in most cases. In the worst-case scenario, legal action would occur against the organization, and depending on the jurisdiction, the supervisor might be liable if he/she is proven to have intentionally harmed the employee. Other damage results may occur, such as loss of leadership credibility, team morale drops (because we know employees share news with their teammates), and of course, employee turnover, which tends to be costly for any organization. I'm sure there are other negative consequences as a result of improper performance reviews one can list, but you get the idea.

The key to addressing ethical responsibilities in the performance appraisals section is to first focus on the actual evaluations of the employee's job performance for the past year or, in some cases, mid-year. Second, the evaluator/supervisor should have prior performance appraisal training in order to do them properly. Lastly, the ethics training must focus on the responsibility of leadership to be "fair and just" by applying and practicing ethical conduct and eliminating any explicit or implied unethical behavior.

Disciplinary Actions:

Similar to performance appraisals, when disciplinary action is performed improperly, the results usually lead to wrongful termination cases, whether in an arbitration hearing, labor commission complaint, or a jury trial. Either way, it is very costly for everyone, plaintiff and defendant. In a nutshell, disciplinary actions include documenting bad performance or behavior (write ups), or correction actions plans, such a Performance Improvement Plan (PIP), and lastly, termination of the employee.

At some point in everyone's lives, I believe a person has been mistreated or knows of others who have been mistreated at work and wrongfully terminated. Some have taken legal actions, while others simply moved on out of fear of future retaliation of other opportunities. However, while there are times in which termination is warranted, the key is to assure the process is legitimately ethical. That means an existing procedure of written warnings, from step one to final step, and of course, a written policy details such steps, etc. Most importantly, leaders need to be trained as to how to conduct disciplinary actions and on the significance of ethical conduct in this area. Again, like performance appraisals, disciplinary actions must be conducted with the intended purpose, which is focusing on job performance and behavior.

During ethical training, the focus must be on fairness, without personal bias and wrongful judgements. Such ethical training should also include examples and/or scenarios of the right and wrong way of implementing disciplinary actions. By the end of the training, the trainees should understand the legal and ethical implications of conducting disciplinary action and have a sense of confidence when faced with an unpleasant situation and disciplinary actions must be taken, it will be conducted accurately.

Favoritism-Free Workplace Environment:

Every employee, supervisor, manager, and executive knows and understands that favoritism is unethical, unprofessional, and simply unproductive, yet sadly, it still exists in the workforce. Some organizations have implemented policies explicitly forbidding favoritism, but like general ethics policy, it is a policy without any training. Again, it is presumed that the leaders know and understand that favoritism has negative impacts on organizations, their teams, and themselves.

What is favoritism? What are the impacts of favoritism? In the workplace environment, favoritism is an act of treating one or a group better than others based on personal bias rather than professional judgment. Examples of such acts include promoting or hiring individuals unqualified for the position over others, giving unjustifiably preferable treatment to a group and excluding others, giving larger percentage salary increases for some but not others without proper cause, and creating opportunities for particular people but excluding others.

As the old saying goes, for every action, there is a reaction, and for leaders who practice favoritism, they eventually create an imbalanced team, department, and even organization. While the favored few are content and happy, the unfavored majority are unhappy, discontented, and disconnected in various ways. When staff are unhappy, their productivity, creative thoughts, and willingness to assist diminish. The end result will be not only turnover of excellent staff, but loss of leadership credibility for leaders who practice favoritism. Once credibility is lost, it is very difficult to rebuild.

Credibility loss has its own consequences, such as damage to professional reputation that can have long-term detriment for future growth in the organization or being selected for higher positions in other organizations. Additionally, if a CEO/President of any organization favors others, it becomes part of the organization's culture, which of course, will have a larger negative impact on the organization and staff. Therefore, it is clear there are unfavorable impacts due to favoritism, and elaborating on it during ethics training would allow leaders to be mindful of favoritism and its consequences.

Development and Promotion:

Part of good leadership is to develop individuals for more advanced positions and might require promotion to a different position, with a different title and coupled with a salary increase. The key to developing others is to recognize their skills, core competencies, but above all, motivation. However, once again, one must be mindful to avoid any personal feelings and favoritism in this area. The areas of development and promotion are critical and, on many occasions, argumentative. It's argumentative because even if the leader rightfully and justifiably promoted one or more staff members, some might argue that they were overlooked and did not get the opportunity to be developed. Unfortunately, this is a common theme among many organizations, and what some organizations have done is create proper processes for development and promotion of employees to assure it is being practiced properly.

There is still room for personal judgment, and this is where the ethical behavior and practice must be applied, even if such leaders follow the development and promotion process perfectly. Therefore, during ethics training, application of ethical conduct must be discussed in the area of development and promotion.

Creating an Open and Honest Environment:

At some point in one's career, he/she will hear statements such as "great place to work, nurturing work environment, or creative atmosphere." On the opposite side, one might also hear statements such as "toxic work environment, horrible place to work, and/or oppressive workplace."

Obviously, all organizations would prefer to be called a great place to work, etc. However, the task of doing so requires more than one action plan. It requires several plans working concurrently or, in other cases, gradually. Therefore, whether one is currently in a toxic work environment or a nurturing one, ethically speaking, as a leader, one must take steps to change and improve the bad work environment or continue to improve the great work place.

Why should creating an open and honest work environment partly fall within the ethics training? Many employees who choose to become leaders are unaware of the higher ethical standards that come with leadership. Most understand the higher responsibilities, but seldom are conscious of the ethical standards. If one begins by creating a great working environment with ethical intentions and actions, it will produce excellent results. It begins with the internal departmental/team communications.

Communication must be open and honest. This means that each staff member should be able to express their opinion and be allowed to give candid feedback regardless of whether it challenges goals of the department or organization. For example, assuming there is an organizational initiative to make a large change and there are prospective negative impacts that might result from this initiative, the staff must be encouraged to communicate their thoughts and concerns. Not only will this assure that such initiative is being deliberately examined, but it is also developing open communication.

Another means of creating an open and honest environment is the ability to give and receive honest feedback, no matter how difficult the subject matter is. Of course, the contrary situation is a closed communication environment, by which leaders put forth plans and expect their staff to follow it without receiving their feedback on projects. This will likely have numerous negative impacts as a result of a closed communication team environment.

There are other action plans for creating a great working environment, and as mentioned previously, it can be implemented concurrently or gradually, but most importantly, it has to begin with ethical purpose and actions in order to be successful.

Accountabilities:

One of the main duties of leadership is holding their staff accountable for job performance and/or professional behavior/conduct. That means staff must follow the appropriate laws, workforce policies and procedures of the organization, and preform their job in accordance with their job description. Failure to do so will most likely result in disciplinary actions which can lead to job termination. However, with such duty to hold staff accountable, leaders must be conscious of their personal responsibilities as leaders. By accepting a leadership role, one has accepted a position that is accompanied by higher standards in ethical conduct, job performance, and compliance to laws, policies, and procedures.

John F. Kennedy once said in his speech: *This Administration intends to be candid about its errors; for a wise man once said: "An error does not become a mistake until you refuse to correct it." We intend to accept full responsibilities for our errors; and we expect you to point them out when we miss them.*

Clearly, President Kennedy's intent was to be honest about any mistakes that might and would occur during his administration, but the overall message was that his administration will be accountable.

What does it mean to be accountable? In a nutshell, being accountable is taking responsibility for one's actions when plans fail. For some, being accountable is very difficult because the results can be damaging. One can be demoted or terminated from their current job. Unfortunately, those individuals rely on a different tactic, and that is blaming others for their mistakes and/or making unjustifiable excuses rather than taking the honest path. Clearly, from an ethical standpoint, the candid approach is the right approach, and while it is tougher and can be more exhausting approach, the results are more favorable in both short and long term.

Hypothetically speaking, assume President Kennedy was aware of numerous mistakes his administration had done, and rather than be candid with the public, he took the dishonest approach and tried hiding the truth. As with many lies, they are eventually discovered, and once it's discovered, the end result would be public distrust, and loss of leadership credibility. Of course, thereafter, any initiative that the President Kennedy put forth would face harsh criticism by the public and other lawmakers, even if the initiative is an excellent plan. Since the president lost public trust and credibility, any attempt to gain it back would be very challenging and the probabilities are unlikely.

However, if the president took the honest approach and acknowledged his administration's mistake and made plans to correct such mistakes (even if it was very difficult), he would have gained more respect and certainly more trust by the public. The challenge of correcting mistakes would be far simpler than the challenge of attempting to regain trust and credibility. Therefore, as during ethics training, leaders must know and understand how and why to be accountable for their actions.

Conclusion:

At some point, leaders of organizations and/or board members will have the necessity to provide leadership training for their staff or current management team, but whether the organization chooses to hire professional trainers or hire internal trainer(s), you must include the Four Facet Approach for developing leadership training.

Chapter 5

I. Through the Good Times and Bad Times

Every seasoned HR professional has lived through the recession of 2008, which began impacting some organizations as early as 2007. HR professionals found themselves laying employees off from their organizations and, in some cases, closing facilities. Some companies went out of business, while other reorganized. Either way, it was a terrible time for everyone. For HR professionals, it was especially disheartening, since most chose the field of HR to be part of a positive, nurturing staff and helping organizations meet their objectives. During recession time, through no fault of the employees, they were being terminated due to financial difficulties of the organization. Naturally, HR had to facilitate the entire process of organization-wide staff reductions, and as anyone can imagine, it was not pleasant.

Throughout time, we've reflected on such moments and asked ourselves: Could we HR professionals have done anything different? Were there some preparations for the worst-case situations, such as the 2008 recession? Most importantly, how do we avoid this misfortune in the future? Unfortunately, while some still remember the impact the 2008 recession had on organizations and their staff, many have forgotten about it, especially since the economy has flourished and organizations are in growth mode again. The job market has been strong, and employees have more choice whom to work for than before. However, history has taught us that no matter how strong the economy is today, there will be a time when the economy will eventually weaken for a period of time. Obviously, business must continue regardless of the current economic status of the country, and organizations must develop contingency plans for such an event.

Ideally, it begins as one of the goals of the board of directors for the organization. Like succession planning, a contingency plan for economic recession is to ensure future operations of the organization, especially during economic difficulties. This plan requires commitment, participation, and a plan of action by the entire executive team. The plan should address the following:

Stability of the organization: The organization must withstand temporary setbacks from decrease of revenue, loss of key personnel, and/or customers. The organization should have solid reserve capital and contingencies for key personnel. (See previous discussion on contingency plans.)

Avoid staff reduction: Not only is staff reduction disheartening for everyone in the organization, but it affects the performance and morale of the current staff for months, if not years. Lack of confidence and distrust of the executive team may occur after staff is reduced, not to mention, public relations issues may arise as well. The executive team should only consider reducing staff as a last resort, which it does not translate to losing profits or maintaining a balanced budget (breaking even), but rather a foreseeable or imminent loss of capital for the whole organization.

Cost-saving approach: The plan should have a tactical approach to saving money, without reducing the quality of customer service or reducing critical benefits for the employee population, such as healthcare, retirement plan, etc. In this area, every department, from operations, finance to HR must find methods of saving money. It starts by reducing waste (as discussed previously under efficiency practices).

Additionally, there is a likelihood that more methods of saving can be achieved, but it takes strategic thought process on this subject by key personnel.

<u>Alternative ways to generate income:</u> Generally speaking, the more diverse the organization's products or services, the more likelihood they can sustain business in a challenging economy. It is rare today to see organizations rely on one product or one service, but some exist. For that one product or one service, organizations that survived the 2008 recession, their product or services were typically strong at the time. However, while some products and services seem timeless, things change, and if organizations are not willing to change and make improvements, they will eventually go out of business. Companies like Kodak lost their market by the digital camera technology and eventually filed bankruptcy, though today, they are trying to provide other services in order be back in prosperous business.

Whatever industry one is in, organizational leaders must consider additional and/or alternative ways for generating business. For instance, some healthcare organizations began providing services other than medical, such as dental, mental health, and even acupuncture.

This allowed them to diversify their services and provide their current patients with variety, while generating additional capital. Others have invested a portion of their reserves into stocks and bonds for the future, similar to that of a 401K for an employee. Therefore, it is always a great idea to find other means of generating business, no matter how strong or weak the economy is at the time.

II. Outside the Scope of HR

In large or small organizations, good HR leadership provides training resources for their staff, whether internal training (in-house) or external training by professional vendors. However, as the focus of training becomes exclusively on HR topics, there are other areas to which HR professionals should be exposed. As each HR leader develops their departmental culture and sets expectations, the one thought process that is important, albeit forgotten at times, is promoting Organizational Thinking by everyone in the staff.

Organizational thinking is a thought process which places the organization's needs and objectives above all others. This is not to say that departmental goals or personal professional goals are not important, but without the survival of the organization, departmental and/or personal professional goals may not be achieved. This thought process requires HR professionals to think outside the scope of HR duties. Not only should HR professionals be active participants, but they should be partnering with other departmental staff to achieve organizational goals.

The benefit of organizational thinking and practice is that it strengthens the value of HR professionals. No longer will HR professionals be known as administrative professionals, but rather as partners for the organization. Some of the areas outside the scope of HR include but are not limited to the following:

<u>Safety:</u> In some organizations, safety is a part of HR since it connects directly with the health and safety of employees. In other organizations, safety falls within the responsibilities of the operational staff, except for managing worker's compensation. In my view, safety is equal partnership with HR and operations. Yes, HR must manage the administrative and financial side of worker's compensation, but it is operations that must assure safety practices are in place.

Every organization must have a safety committee(s), or a similar forum, which should be managed by key HR and operational staff. Such staff should include both management and non-management personnel. Non-management personnel are essential members to the committee, since they are the ones working directly in operations and, most likely, are the ones who will spot safety hazards. Additionally, an organization must have a comprehensive safety plan, which should include safety training, safety practices, emergency response, and proper reporting, as well as an organization safety policy and procedure that details guidelines, practices, and enforcement. HR, operations, and perhaps even compliance professionals must assure such policies are up to date and properly executed.

Vendor Management: Most organizations and their departments have multiple vendors working on their behalf. They serve a strategic operational need, and of course, they can be very costly. Vendors' services vary from software companies to benefit brokers and more, but most importantly, they provide services which organizations cannot perform in-house. However, vendor management has become a priority for many organizations because many vendors made performance promises they failed to keep. Such promises include but are not limited to excellent customer service, products functioning as intended, timely deliveries, problem solving, accountability, and overall customer care.

Since HR regularly utilizes vendors for their human resource information system (HRIS), and for other systems, such as recruitment, training, etc., HR must hold these vendors accountable to the expectation they set to HR and their organization by providing the services they agreed upon in contract. On many occasions, there are glitches in the system and may affect the work of the department, which, at times, are reasonable and understandable. However, when such glitches and other malfunctions become a regular occurrence, it is not acceptable. The lack of vendor operations will reflect on the HR department's abilities with the employee populations of the organization.

In such situations, HR must take the necessary steps to address these occurrences with the vendor, giving the vendor the opportunity to create a plan of action, with reasonable time of completion, in order to avoid future occurrences. HR must be prepared for the worst-case scenario and have a contingency plan if vendor fails to deliver. Lastly, HR should maintain some communication with staff and the leadership team on such issues; it will result in greater understanding by everyone.

Vendor management should be the responsibility of every department, HR, finance, operations, and other. Some organizations have specific staff that manages vendors, for which they keep track of expired contracts and assure compliance and more. Unfortunately, such staff cannot evaluate the performance of these vendors. In fact, each department that uses the services of vendors are the only ones who can determine whether such vendors are performing in accordance with the signed agreements.

<u>Public Relations:</u> Rarely will you ever see or hear HR is involved in public relations (PR) matters, especially outside the organization. In most cases, organizations have individuals or a department specializing in the area of public relations, which, of course, is ideal. PR specialists are responsible for growing and maintaining the organization's brand by various mass public communications. PR is designed not only to keep

the public informed, but to highlight the organization's strengths and values.

On the other hand, HR has a small public relations role, but not as extensive as those who specialize in PR. For instance, for prospective talent hired for the organization, strategic public relations recruitment is utilized in the job ads and public recruitment appearances by members of HR. In these areas, it is critical to highlight the strength of the organization's brand and values. Moreover, it allows HR to promote other benefits for the prospective talent, such as growth opportunities, great place to work, and more.

Additionally, excellent HR professionals (especially at the senior level) are known to be tactful communicators. Some might refer to them as the diplomats of the organization partly because such HR professionals are regularly attempting to resolve issues by finding middle-ground agreements with both parties. It might be between an employee and their manager, between union and management, or general mediation between parties. Naturally, as diplomats of the organization, these HR professionals usually will attend functions on behalf of the organization and represent the organization in the same manner as the CEO. Building relations and networking with other organizations and its professionals are common public relations practices for CEO and some of the executive team, yet it has only been in the last few years that HR has become more involved in this area. While this duty is not typically expressed in any HR job descriptions, it is a necessary duty for HR professionals to fulfill.

<u>Wellness:</u> Typically, wellness falls under the responsibilities of HR, except for some organizations which elect to manage it separately, even though wellness has been in the HR world over a decade now. The main reason for including wellness in the category of outside the scope of HR is that many HR professionals are not trained, practice, or understand wellness.

Wellness for organizations includes programs designed to transform and improve the health of the employees in the workforce. Study after study confirms that healthy employees are happy and productive employees. Nonetheless, creating wellness programs is not a small undertaking, especially since there are many misconceptions about wellness. Some employees believe wellness programs are aimed to guilt/force staff to eat more vegetables and fruits only. Others think they will be forced to have medical examinations completed, from which organizations will have access to private information and utilize it negatively. Of course, none of these beliefs is accurate, especially the medical examinations.

Wellness programs are an additional benefit for the employee population of the organization, and it is a purely volunteer participation program. Sponsored by the organization and led by staff, the wellness program should generally consist of nutritional education, sponsored physical activities, health club discounts, cost saving meal preparation ideas, and incentives and rewards for establishing and meeting wellness objectives. Obviously, a wellness committee must be established with its own budget to be managed by committee members or a wellness committee chairperson.

Like safety, wellness should be part of HR's duties since it directly affects the health of the employees. Certainly, HR should be an equal partner with other organizational professionals, not only to help establish a wellness committee, but to assist with managing its functions. A charter should be created by committee members, with clear guidelines for all employees to follow. Lastly, many organizations today have great wellness ideas and programs which other can utilize without reinventing it. At the end of the day, it is about the overall health of staff, and whatever means organizations can support it, HR should always be involved.

III. Pitfalls in HR

Those who have been in HR for years understand that the HR field is not an exact science. While many of us in HR leadership have applied certain HR principles similarly, we all have taken different approaches in other HR areas. Regardless of the industry, many HR leaders throughout the year have fallen unconsciously into complacency, which, unfortunately, tends to lead to mediocrity. For some, mediocrity is acceptable, especially for those who do not work in a competitive environment. Others see mediocrity as the enemy of forward thinking and innovation. From my perspective, mediocrity has many detrimental effects one can list. However, the one which stands out the most is if a leader accepts mediocrity, he/she will limit the full potential of the staff to reach great heights and deprive the organization or other organizations from a great leader in HR.

<u>Evading Complacency:</u> It is easy to tell someone to not be satisfied with everything, it is another to explain how to avoid it. First, there is nothing wrong with being satisfied with the completion of a project or a current HR process. However, every process, project, or any other HR function should have annual review dates to evaluate its effectiveness, efficiency, and maintain awareness of becoming complacent. Second, avoid any lazy behavior, especially in view of your staff. Staff can be very emotionally sophisticated, and they

will usually sense such behavior and might follow it. Third, create a standard of excellence for the HR department, and lastly, maintain reasonable high energy level for the entire HR team.

<u>Lack of Flexibility:</u> In some organizations, all levels of leadership refer to the HR department as the "NO department," a label which most HR professionals (including myself) find unpleasant. Many believe it is because HR is typically firm on compliance issues that relate to organization's policies and employment law. In truth, this is not the case. Being firm on compliance issues is part of HR's duties and ethical obligation to the organization. The main reason for the "NO department" label the perception of lack of flexibility by the HR department, anything from HR processes to personnel matters.

Case in point, in efforts to attempt to move processes faster to fulfill the business needs, managers often find HR professionals unwilling to compromise or make exceptions. On the other side, HR professionals argue that once they compromise or make exceptions, it sets expectations, and soon after, the exceptions to the rule become the rule of operation. Ultimately, it will have negative impacts on the structure of any processes. One thing to recognize is that both HR professionals and organizational managers are performing their jobs in the best interest of their department and organization, and any impression that such professional is acting in their own interest is false. This is why there are always arrangements that can be made for a "happy medium" solution.

First, let's consider the common objectives of both HR and organizational managers. It is basically assisting the organization with meeting its business goals. Second, both must have an understanding of the importance of each other's work challenges and recognize neither one is more important than the other. Third, develop an agreement in which, if exception must be made, it must not lead to regular practice. Each case is different than another, and rational judgements must be applied to each one. Fourth, proper documentation is necessary to maintain historical practices, especially with making exceptions. Lastly, going back to our discussion of the annual reviews of HR processes and functions, if such tasks are properly performed, it would reduce the constant inquiries for making exceptions and compromises on HR functions and processes.

Organizational management certainly has many challenges to fulfill, and many understand HR is a support department designed to assist them. Frequently, organizational management tends to forget that HR is their partner in business, though at times, HR professionals are treated with less regard. However, before labeling HR as the "NO department," managers at all levels should consider some self-reflection and ask themselves whether their management style is reasonable and cooperative or forceful, demanding, unwilling to compromise, and condescending. Obviously, the more cooperative the style of management one has, the more likely true partnerships will be created with others.

For HR professionals, one important note to remember in this category is to avoid being rigid. Before declining a request(s), take the time and listen to all the details. If you find that the request(s) is unreasonable or defies policies and other protocols, offer alternative solutions for such unreasonable request(s) before declining the original request(s). On many occasions, the manager may not receive exactly what he/she has requested, but with the assistance of HR, there might be other ways to achieve the manager's overall objectives by various thoughtful ideas. By offering alternative means, it creates better working partnerships with management, and hopefully, eliminates any thoughts of the "NO department."

<u>Uncontrolled Emotions:</u> If only human beings could fully control our emotions at all times during work, it would probably reduce the amount of conflict and allow for more cooperation. Unfortunately, we humans are created with multiple emotions, from positive ones to negative ones. The other side is that having passion for creating, building, leading, teaching others, and overall contributing to society is very positive.

On the negative side, the most problematic emotions for HR professionals (especially HR leadership) are anger, condescending behavior, emotional outburst, assuming personal attack when constructive feedback is given, and flying off the handle while constructive feedback is given.

I realize these are behavioral science issues, and those who are in the profession of mental health are more qualified to make recommendations as to how to control negative emotions in the work environment. However, basic behavioral sciences have taught us that everything begins with awareness. Many times, those HR professionals who act on these negative emotions are usually not aware of their action at the time, and unfortunately, they do have long-term negative impact on others, especially their direct coworkers and staff. Being aware of these negative emotions and avoiding them is a matter of recognizing the problem, making a conscious effort to abstain, and maintaining discipline throughout each workday. However, if self-help does not work, it's time to see a mental health provider, because most will agree that such behaviors are unproductive, disheartening, and simply unacceptable.

Jeopardizing reputation: There's an old saying, "We live in a small world." Of course, this statement means something different to each. For our purpose, it means that the HR world is very small. How one performs his/her duties, behaves under different circumstances, and works with others carries to the next job, regardless of the industry. In other words, HR professionals develop a reputation at any level, from administrative to strategic.

Professional reputations are vital in the professional world, no matter how great one's contributing skills. It is the one element which can provide a professional with more and/or better opportunities or limit opportunities entirely. Of course, this would depend on each professional and their actions. For example, throughout the years, there have been many strong skilled, well-educated HR professionals, yet some of those professionals have developed combative and uncooperative attitudes with their coworkers and staff. Otherwise, some have made erroneous decisions without proper examination of the issues, which eventually caused harm to the organization. Ultimately, the result of such actions damaged the reputation of these individuals, which caused some of these HR professionals to leave HR entirely.

The importance of a professional reputation is understated and underestimated. Unfortunately, it is something we are not teaching our staff or the upcoming young professionals of tomorrow. Like etiquette, it is presumed that all parents are teaching their children as we are presuming those in higher education or the professional world are teaching the young upcoming professionals. The benefits of a strong professional reputation are considerable, but while HR professionals are building their reputation, they must stay away from certain pitfalls that would damage their reputation entirely.

Some of these pitfalls have previously been mentioned, such as uncooperative and combative attitude and making erroneous decisions without proper due diligence. However, the one which is the most problematic is the Crusader HR professional. While this HR professional intends to advocate for fairness, express strong opinions, and make recommendations, the pitfall occurs when this HR professional becomes relentless with his/her advocacy, expressed communications, and recommendations.

Ethically speaking, HR professionals have a duty to advocate for fairness and make recommendations. Nonetheless, when advocacy become an obsession, with unreasonably and overwhelming communications, such an HR professional has undermined their professional reputation. The main reason is this behavior tends to demonstrate a lack of compromise, an inability to work in the middle ground, or HR terminology, work in the gray areas. Naturally, the gray is the middle ground of black and white, with the black and white referring to the two opposing extremes.

Lastly, we have all worked for a terrible boss at some point in our careers, and we have detailed stories about how this boss treated us. Naturally, we all wished the organization would have terminated this person, at least taken notice to his/her behavior. Unfortunately, on many occasions, organizations fail to act, and leave the employee with one option: to resign from their position and find another job elsewhere. Of course, this situation occurs regularly in our country, but where the pitfall may happen is how the employee resigns.

If an employee is resigning under stressful and discontented conditions, he/she may resign without proper notice (minimum two weeks), or worse, expressing anger during same-day resignation. Unfortunately, while the employee may feel justified by this resignation, it will have its drawbacks. Prospective employers might discover such resignation facts through reference check of the previous employer and will likely not offer the position. Generally speaking, most employers frown upon this behavior because they consider it unprofessional. If prospective employers have other strong candidates for one position, and likelihood doing the process of elimination, it takes one negative element in a candidate's background to be eliminated from considerations. Therefore, if faced with this situation, apply discipline and follow the professional protocols for job resignation.

IV. Glimpse into the Future of HR

If you ask every HR expert in the US about the future of HR, I would imagine most will talk about the changing business world, the labor market, technological innovations, and the impact of political actions. With such information, and hopefully good data, these experts can make reasonable predictions of HR. On the other hand, for those of us who have been in the frontlines of HR operations for more than a quarter of a century may have other views, including from each other.

From my perspective, I see HR facing many challenges, as they always have. Some might be different, while other challenges might be the same. In the next few years, there is a likelihood that we will enter into a recession (according to some economists), which as I discussed previously, has its issues. Another is the upcoming new generation entering the HR world, with a different set of values and expectations from the current and past generations.

Let's begin with a scenario that occurred some time ago. In the last few years, it has been an "employee market," which means the employment opportunities have been strong for job seekers such that organizations have been struggling to fill positions with the qualified candidates. On most occasions, they have compromised by hiring beginners who have the potential to be trained into the position. Naturally, the salary offered for these candidates is usually the minimum amount of the organization's salary range, which is usually in accordance to market value, budgetary requirements, or both. The lowest salary is typically offered to the least experience candidates, and of course, the more years of experience one has, the higher salary offered.

However, while this is a standard practice for most organizations, some of these new generation candidates have declined such offers. Some of these candidates have counter offered with an unreasonable amount which reflected a more experienced professional in the field. Obviously, such counter offers were declined by HR simply because these candidates did not meet the level of qualifications for such salaries. When explained to this new generation candidates the reason for minimum salary range offers, and the benefit opportunities it comes with, such as learning and developing new skills and opportunity to develop experience, the overwhelming reaction was not constructive. Most understood the rationale behind the offered salary yet persisted in arguing their potential to accomplish at a higher level. Organizations must recognize such potential and offer higher salaries.

Unfortunately, this scenario is not an isolated incident, nor it is an epidemic one. It is, however, reflective of the times we've lived in the last fifteen years or so. In the late 1990s, during an interview with Michael Jordan (MJ), he expressed his concerns over talented players receiving larger contracts and sponsorships from various companies before stepping on the court and playing their first professional game. MJ's argument is, by rewarding players for their potential, it takes the incentive away from working for hard for such rewards. In their time, Michael Jordan, Magic Johnson, and Larry Bird had to accomplish great things before receiving any sponsorships or larger contracts. Today, the practice and mindset are different than the past, and unfortunately, it has spread to other areas of employment.

Other generational differences that many HR professionals have observed are the level of ambition in the current versus the new generation. During college site recruitments, most potential candidates of this new generation were looking for work but emphasized "work/life balance" priorities, which, of course, means something different to each. When asked, what it meant to them to have work/life balance, the general answer was to work to enjoy life and activities outside of work. Most were not interested in management positions or didn't have any other motivation to excel in their careers.

Also, most were not willing to relocate or commute any distance for a great opportunity. There was a small percentage that were accomplishment driven and had aspirations to do more in their careers, much like the past and current generation.

While I do believe in balance, regardless whether it's between work and outside personal interests, it has to be up to each to create such balance, but without compromising one's strong work ethic and the desires to achieve. My concern for the future of HR is whether the new generation of HR professionals is prepared for the daily challenges HR faces, from resolving conflicts to working long hours and weekends on many occasions. Also, there is a concern whether this new generation has the passion, discipline, and the drive to excel in the HR field and adopt it as a long-term career.

There is one possibility that concerns me most. Can this new generation cope with working in HR during a recession by assisting management with choices as to who and how many employees will be laid off from work? Although such concerns are valid and certainly challenging, there are proactive solutions, but it must be accomplished by the participation of the current generation of HR professionals. As seasoned HR professionals, we must assist the next generation of professionals to make HR better than it is now.

It is our job to teach them to prepare for the worse times and celebrate the good ones. Most importantly, we need to motivate them to be better than us.

I am hopeful for the future of HR and foresee good changes, even with upcoming expected or unforeseen challenges. Yes, I am generally optimistic, yet how can any human being desire and expect positive outcomes in life and not be optimistic? If changes for the better must be made, it cannot start with pessimism. The negative emotions alone will drain the energy out of any attempt at progress.

V. Moments of Reflection

Generally speaking, after retirement, most professionals take the time and reflect upon their careers, from the good times to the bad, but hopefully, it is mostly good. You might hear moments of great achievement, working with great people, or unfortunately sad moments in which people have suffered in their career. While it is depressing, nonetheless, it is part of our reality in life. Certainly, in my career, I've had many bad times and situations, and I have reflected upon them only to use them as learning moments. It is pointless to dwell on negative situations without a plan of action to move ahead and overcome such bad situations.

I decided a long time ago to reflect on the good and the bad situations regularly for a few reasons:

1) To take a deep breath and let things settle down, especially while in the moments of difficult and unusual situations.
2) To find learning moments from every situation.
3) To create strategies or new approaches for such difficult situations.
4) Above all, to take time to reflect upon the successes of the team, yourself, and others in the organization.

If I were to retire today, what moments would I reflect upon? I think I would reflect upon the relationships that I built throughout the years working in HR, from staff, colleagues, and others outside the organization who partnered with me on various projects. All these wonderful individuals became not only working partners, but friends through the years. Still today, most of my previous staff members, colleagues, and others, including bosses, maintain some contact and communication with me through various social media resources.

Certainly, with each of these individuals, I can look back on moments working together, facing and overcoming challenges, while enjoying a few laughs together. Some professionals have referred to people they work with as a family. Well, it is understandable, given the fact that people working together spend over 40 hours a week with each other, much more than the amount of time they spend with their own families. With such a large amount of time spent with each other, one is bound to develop relationships.

It is because of HR that allowed me to meet great professionals and develop relationships with many diverse individuals. Unlike any other department in the organization, only HR has and must have working relationships with all other departments and their personnel in the organization. Such gives HR a distinctive position in the organization, and whether it is liked or disliked by others, it is, nonetheless, a vital element of an organization's structure. From my perspective, I would encourage others to select human resources as a career path, but I would also encourage others to think it through. While HR is very challenging, it can also be very rewarding. That, of course, would depend on each's rewarding expectations.

Acknowledgements

It began as a journey by a husband, his wife, and their two boys migrating to United States from Baghdad, Iraq, sacrificing their good jobs, family ties, and comforts in effort to give their boys a better life and hopefully provide them opportunities for their future. Naturally, as new immigrants to the country, no real assistance was available, and adaptabilities were discovered through trial and error. With hard work, determination, and the will to provide a better life for their children, my parents attended and completed various technical schools which allowed them decent jobs while avoiding any public assistance. My parents taught me strong work ethics, the principles of doing, but above all, they provided me with unconditional support toward any goals that I have in my life. Without them, I would not have accomplished anything, especially this book.

I would also like to acknowledge those who made an impact in my journey. I would like to acknowledge some of my professors and staff members at Sierra College, California State University, Sacramento, and New College of California Law School. Thank you for always being there and supporting me during some of my tough academic challenges.

In my professional life, I have worked in great organizations, and they provided me with opportunities to learn and be the professional that I am today. Moreover, they provided me with wonderful staff, great colleagues, and fair-minded superiors. It has been an honor and a pleasure working with such organizations and their staff.

Lastly, I am honored to acknowledge my extended family (cousins and all), recent close friends, longtime friends who I met through odd jobs during college, bodybuilding/fitness world, and social gatherings. Your confidence and support of all my endeavors have been greatly appreciated through the years. Thank you.

About the Author

Sam Altawil has spent the last 25 years in the field of human resources, with the last 17 years focusing on leadership roles. He is a seasoned HR professional with varying levels of industry experience, from manufacturing, consulting, and most recently, healthcare. As a young man, Sam earned his bachelor's degree in Social Sciences from California State University, Sacramento and completed his Juris Doctorate from New College of California, Law School, one of the oldest public interest law schools in the US.

Having a reputation for getting the job done, Sam has been offered and accepted challenging positions for organizations that provided him with opportunities to achieve under difficult circumstances. During such, Sam was able to learn many of the facets of HR while adapting to unforeseeable difficult events, while elevating and developing members of HR to their full potential. His colleagues have always credited Sam for being a great supportive partner, diplomatic communicator, being compassionate, with an ability to stay composed under pressure.

In more recent years, Sam was the Director of Human Resources for two outstanding Federally Qualified Health Care Centers that were dedicated to severing the underprivileged. In his leadership role, Sam utilized his methodology to improve what once was considered to be broken HR departments. In 2013, Sam won "Best HR Practice" in one of the sturdiest Federal audits performed by the Health Resources and Services Administration (HRSA). In 2015, 2016 Sam and his HR team guided the organization to win "Best Place to Work" status in the North Bay Business Journal.

Today, Sam continues his journey in HR, constantly striving to find innovative avenues for improvements. His belief has always been, if human beings created something, there are always opportunities for improvements. A thought shared by his hero, Bruce Lee.

www.ingramcontent.com/pod-product-compliance
Lightning Source LLC
Chambersburg PA
CBHW070230180526
45158CB00001BA/318